DISCARD

50+ US Black Women in STEM

CHANGING
THE
EQUATION

TONYA BOLDEN

ABRAMS BOOKS FOR YOUNG READERS
NEW YORK

Cataloging-in-Publication Data has been applied for
and may be obtained from the Library of Congress.

ISBN 978-1-4197-0734-6

Text copyright © 2020 Tonya Bolden
Edited by Howard W. Reeves
Book design by Sara Corbett
For image credits, see page 198.

Printed and bound in China
10 9 8 7 6 5 4 3

Abrams Books for Young Readers are available at special discounts when
purchased in quantity for premiums and promotions as well as fundraising
or educational use. Special editions can also be created to specification.
For details, contact specialsales@abramsbooks.com or the address below.

Abrams® is a registered trademark of Harry N. Abrams, Inc.

ABRAMS The Art of Books
195 Broadway, New York, NY 10007
abramsbooks.com

CONTENTS

ALPHA

During her 2001–2004 tenure in a leadership position at the National Science Foundation (NSF), white biologist Dr. Judith Ramaley took a shine to the acronym STEM.

Science.
Technology.
Engineering.
Mathematics.

The NSF, a federal agency that funds education and research in specified fields, had previously used SMET (Science, Math, Engineering, Technology). Dr. Ramaley championed the shift from SMET to STEM, she said, "because science and math support the other two disciplines and because STEM sounds nicer than SMET." Too, SMET "subtly implies that science and math came first or were better. The newer term suggests a meaningful connection among them."

With STEM, the NSF doesn't include physicians and some other medical professionals. Understandable. When the SMET, then STEM push began, the nation had no shortage of doctors, for example. This was not the case with other fields, such as engineering.

Pinning down STEM is a bit tricky. For example, the US Department of Labor's Bureau of Labor Statistics considers nursing a STEM field, but the NSF does not. And while the NSF lists certain social sciences as STEM (psychology, for example), the Department of Commerce does not.

Hmm.

When it comes to history, many people take a broad view of STEM. I am one of them. Just as in an overview of technology I wouldn't start with the mainframe computer (and omit the wheel and the Gutenberg press), so *Changing the Equation: 50+ US Black Women in STEM* includes physicians, for example, such as the first woman you will meet in the book: Dr. Rebecca Crumpler. She earned her MD in 1864—four years before black people in America had citizenship, six years before black men had the right to the national vote, and fifty-six years before America's women had that right, too.

How can we not honor the pioneers in science, technology, engineering, and mathematics—women who in their day were cutting-edge? Women who didn't have access to the sort of education that would allow them to enter some now NSF-approved STEM field? Women like Dr. Crumpler blazed a trail for others in this book whose contributions and/or personal stories also called to me, intrigued me, piqued my curiosity.

Women such as biochemist Marie Maynard Daly, computer scientist (and more!) Donna Auguste, industrial engineer Pamela McCauley, chemical engineer Paula T. Hammond, geologist and micropaleontologist Lisa D. White, cybersecurity pro Emma Garrison-Alexander, and aerospace engineer Aprille Joy Ericsson.

In these profiles (some short, some longish) and in quick mentions (in **boldface**), you will encounter women with an array of academic degrees, including two kinds of doctors: those with medical degrees (MDs) and those with doctorates, aka PhDs—the highest academic degree possible. Some degrees were earned at historically black colleges and universities such as Hampton, Howard, and Tuskegee, others at majority-white institutions such as Columbia, Cornell, Harvard, and MIT.

In the pages of this book you just might find role models, inspirations. You might also rethink a field you once dismissed as something you would *never* do. Or be able to do. Maybe, too, you'll discover a vocation you did not know existed and think, *Hmm, maybe that's for me!*

PhD, the abbreviation for the Latin *philosophiae doctor*, "doctor of philosophy," is awarded in a range of fields, from English to Engineering. "Philosophy" here is used in the broadest sense of the Greek **philosophía** (φιλοσοφία), meaning "love of wisdom." "Doctor" descends from the Latin *docere*: "to teach." MD is the abbreviation for the Latin *medicinae doctor*: "teacher of medicine."

▶ POS•SI•BIL•I•TIES: Unidentified woman circa 1899. In the nineteenth century, careers in STEM were becoming a reality for black women.

PART 1

In the Vanguard

n early America the rap was that black people and women were not equipped for STEM.

Unfit.

Too weak.

Lacking the mental muscle.

Blah, blah, blah.

This balderdash persisted into the nineteenth century and beyond.

A black woman's place, said society, was in the cotton or rice fields, in domestic service, or in taking care of her own home and family.

Defiant and determined, a number of black women pushed back against stereotype.

In the early days most black women with a STEM bent became medical doctors. These women were gold in their communities because many white physicians would not treat black people (or treated them badly). Black women were especially grateful for black medicine women because male MDs—regardless of race or ethnicity—could be rather condescending toward female patients.

For STEM-minded black women, teaching was a wide-open field—that is, in schools for black people when segregation reigned by custom, then by law. Some black women became teachers because they were barred from such jobs as, say, researcher at a pharmaceutical company. For others, teaching was a first choice—a prime way to fortify their communities, ready the next generation for success.

REBECCA DAVIS LEE CRUMPLER

1831–1895 • General Practitioner

Soft Bones." "Burns and Scalds." "Diphtheria." "Brain Fever."

These are some of the ailments and diseases explored in *A Book of Medical Discourses* (1883) by Rebecca Crumpler, the first US black woman to earn a medical degree. The year was 1864.

Never mind that many white people back then deemed blackness a handicap.

Never mind that many men deemed womanhood a handicap.

Never mind that many women and men, regardless of race and ethnicity, deemed doctoring men's work.

Never mind all that! Rebecca surely must have said to herself when she set out to be a physician. This was after eight years as a nurse, mostly in Charlestown, Massachusetts, not yet part of Boston.

America had no nursing schools at the time. Nurses learned by *doing,* and Rebecca

In 1860, of America's 54,543 licensed physicians, 300 were women.

was apparently a gifted medical professional. Armed with great recommendations from male physicians for whom she had worked, at age twenty-eight, she enrolled in Boston's New-England Female Medical College, the world's first medical school for women. It was in March 1864 that this school declared Rebecca (and three other women) a "Doctress of Medicine."

▲ **A WOMAN'S PLACE:** The New-England Female Medical College as it was when Rebecca Crumpler was a student there. In 1874 it merged with the Boston University School of Medicine.

Rebecca's MD came with "OB-GYN training," wrote reporter Edgar B. Herwick III in a piece on Crumpler that included an interview with Doug Hughes, a twenty-first-century dean at the Boston University School of Medicine. Herwick added that in Rebecca's day obstetrics and gynecology was "something few, if any, other medical schools were teaching at the time."

Obstetrics (the study of pregnancy and childbirth) derives from the Latin word for midwife, *obstetrix* (literally a woman who stands opposite a pregnant woman). The Greek **gunē** (γυνή) meaning "female" + **logia**, a Latinization of the Greek **logos** (λόγος), meaning "the study of" = gynecology (the study of the female reproductive system). The shorthand OB-GYN or OBGYN came into vogue around 1960.

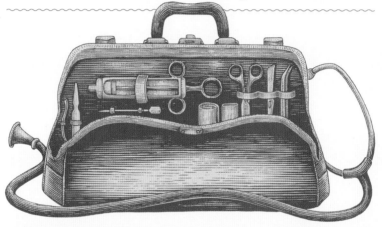

▲ **TOOLS OF THE TRADE:** A contemporary engraving of a nineteenth-century MD's bag.

Rebecca Crumpler, MD, began her practice in Boston; then, "desiring a larger scope for general information, I travelled toward the British Dominion" (Canada). She returned to the States at the close of the Civil War, which resulted in the end of chattel slavery in America. The war also left much of the South in ruin and reeking of renewed white rage against black people and Northerners.

Despite the potential peril a black Northerner faced in the South, Dr. Crumpler went down to Richmond, Virginia, the former Confederate capital. She was eager to be of service to her people and to beef up her knowledge of diseases that afflicted women and children in particular. Working with organizations such as the Freedmen's Bureau, a social service agency set up by Congress, the intrepid Dr. Crumpler medically ministered to scores of Richmond's black residents, many in desperate need of decent food, clothing, and shelter along with health care.

As Dr. Crumpler healed and helped, there were snakes along the way, adders in her path. "Hospitals would not admit her patients; druggists would not fill her prescriptions or sell her supplies," said BU's Doug Hughes. Mean-spirited people joked that the MD behind Crumpler's name stood for "mule driver."

Never mind all that!

Rebecca Crumpler kept on healing, kept on helping.

"She gets the school to send medicine and bandages down by train to Richmond," said Hughes. "And for four or five years she takes care of [black people] under deplorable conditions." Those conditions were ripe for diseases such as typhoid fever and malaria, both of which Rebecca herself contracted.

When this general practitioner returned to Boston, she resumed private practice with "renewed vigor," she wrote. Home and office was in the largely black section of Beacon Hill (the North Slope). When patients had little or no money for office visits and house calls—

Never mind all that!

Rebecca Crumpler, MD, kept on healing, kept on helping.

For a number of years Dr. Crumpler's home and office in Boston was at 67 Joy Street, now a stop on the Boston Women's Heritage Trail.

An internet search will likely result in images said to be of Dr. Crumpler. But historians remain on the hunt for a verified sketch, engraving, or photograph. In the meantime we make do with written descriptions like that in the July 22, 1894, *Boston Daily Globe*.

This newspaper said that Dr. Crumpler, then in her sixties, was "a very pleasant and intellectual woman, and an indefatigable church worker." She was "tall and straight, with light brown skin and gray hair." This much-admired medicine woman died eight months later. By then home was about ten miles south of Boston, in the village of Hyde Park.

The little we know about Dr. Crumpler's youth includes that she was born free in a slave state (Delaware) and raised mostly by an aunt in a free state (Pennsylvania). That aunt was someone whose "usefulness with the sick was continually sought," the doctor recalled in *A Book of Medical Discourses.* This book, based on Crumpler's journals and years of experience, is one of the first, if not the first, published medical text by a black American.

On July 28, 1868, four years after Rebecca Crumpler became an MD, she, along with nearly 5 million other black people in America (roughly 12 percent of the population), became a US citizen when the Fourteenth Amendment was added to the Constitution. The amendment defined citizens as people—other than Native Americans living on reservations—born or naturalized in the United States. (At the time only white people could become naturalized citizens.)

REBECCA J. COLE

1846–1922 • General Practitioner

FIRST

✳ Black graduate of the Female Medical College of Pennsylvania in Philadelphia (later the Woman's Medical College of Pennsylvania) and second US black female MD (1867).

LEGACY

✳ Worked at Lower Manhattan's New York Infirmary for Indigent Women and Children, founded in the 1850s by white British-born Elizabeth Blackwell and her sister, Emily. (Elizabeth was the first woman to graduate from an American med school: Geneva Medical College in Upstate New York, in 1848.) At the New York Infirmary Rebecca Cole's duties included home visits to give women guidance on pre- and postnatal care along with tips on general hygiene. Dr. Cole later cofounded a center in Philadelphia that provided free medical and legal services to women in dire straits.

BACKSTORY

✳ "Determine the base and altitude of an equilateral triangle that contains an area of 1⅖ acres." This was one of ten geometry questions on Rebecca Cole's senior exam at Philadelphia's Institute for Colored Youth (now Cheyney University), her springboard to med school. The exam also had questions on plane and spherical trigonometry along with exercises in two classical languages, Greek and Latin. On a scale of 10 Rebecca averaged 7.24 in mathematics and 9.18 in classical languages. When she graduated from the Institute in 1863, there was only one other young woman in her class and three young men.

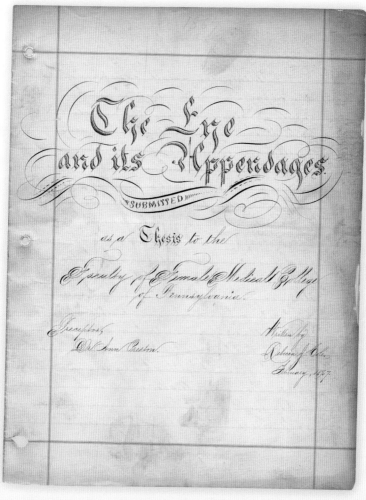

▲ **A WOMAN'S WORK:** The cover page of Dr. Rebecca J. Cole's med school thesis, *The Eye and Its Appendages.*

HALLE TANNER DILLON JOHNSON

1864–1901 • General Practitioner & Institution Builder

FIRST

✳ Woman to pass Alabama's medical exam and become licensed to practice in that state. On September 22, 1891, under the headline "A Colored Female Doctor," the *New York Times* reported that this exam was "an unusually severe one" and that Halle passed it "with a high average." The ten-day exam (taken in August 1891) consisted of four to ten questions in each of ten disciplines. They included Hygiene, Anatomy, and Physical Diagnosis. Example: "Differentiate Pneumonia, Pleuritis, and Bronchitis, by giving the physical signs peculiar to each." The questions (typed) and the answers (in longhand) run more than one hundred pages.

LEGACY

✳ Resident physician for nearly ten years at Alabama's Tuskegee Institute (now University), headed by Booker T. Washington, who had been born into slavery.

✳ Founder of Tuskegee Institute's nursing program and a clinic for locals.

BACKSTORY

✳ Born in Pittsburgh, Pennsylvania, but raised mostly in Philadelphia, she came from a family of high achievers. It included her father, the eminent African Methodist Episcopal Church minister Benjamin Tucker Tanner, and her older brother Henry Ossawa Tanner, renowned artist.

✳ When Halle went to med school, she was a widow and the mother of a three-year-old daughter.

▲ **HALLE THE HEALER:** Halle Tanner Dillon Johnson with fellow members of the Class of 1891 at the Woman's Medical College of Pennsylvania in Philadelphia, in this cherished but damaged photograph. Halle is in the back row, far right, in an outfit with asymmetrical buttons.

ELIZA ANNA GRIER

1864–1902 • Obstetrician-Gynecologist

Dear Friend, . . .

I am a Negro woman. . . . I have been attending [Fisk University in Nashville, Tennessee] for seven years and God willing it, I hope to complete the Advanced Normal Course of study here next June. I desire to be of the most possible benefit to my race and to my fellow creatures. I think I can accomplish more by having a Medical education. . . . I have no money and no source from which to get it only as I work for every dollar. . . .

This letter from twenty-six-year-old Eliza Anna Grier to the Woman's Medical College of Pennsylvania (WMCP) is dated December 6, 1890. In 1891 Eliza Anna, born into slav-

▲ **RESOLUTE:** Dr. Eliza Anna Grier, circa 1897, the year she graduated from med school at age thirty-three.

ery in North Carolina, graduated from Fisk. She then taught at Haines Institute in Augusta, Georgia, a school founded by freeborn black educator Lucy Craft Laney.

In 1893 Eliza Anna's highest hope came true. She was admitted to WMCP. As at Fisk, she had to work while in med school because WMCP's financial aid didn't cover all her expenses.

What people once called a "normal school" we call a teacher's college today.

Some sources say that Eliza Anna alternated a year of school with a year of picking cotton. But where in America does cotton grow year-round to be picked? And there's this: When Grier entered WMCP in 1893, earning an MD was a four-year program. Given that she graduated in 1897, she could not have taken any years off.

This is not to say that getting through med school wasn't a struggle financially. Responding to an 1898 inquiry about

On May 18, 1896, the year before Dr. Grier graduated from med school, in its *Plessy v. Ferguson* decision the US Supreme Court ruled that racial segregation, aka Jim Crow, was constitutional. Treatment of black Americans as second-class citizens became more intense. Colleges and universities could now legally refuse to admit black people. Hospitals, clinics, and physicians could freely refuse to treat black people or do so only in facilities rarely if ever equal to those for white people.

Two months after the *Plessy* decision, in July 1896, two powerful black women's organizations—the National Federation of Afro-American Women (founded in Boston) and the National League of Colored Women (founded in Washington, DC)—joined forces to create the National Association of Colored Women (NACW, today's National Association of Colored Women's Clubs or NACWC). With its motto "Lifting as We Climb," NACW improved the quality of life for black people through educational, cultural, and charitable activities. NACW also crusaded for an end to Jim Crow and for women to have the right to the national vote.

▲ **SOS:** The start of
Dr. Grier's March 7, 1901,
letter to Susan B. Anthony.

Eliza Anna's standing at WMCP, Dean Clara Marshall replied that it was "respectable." She added that it was hard to say "how much better work she would have done had she not been constantly harassed by want of adequate means of support."

Dr. Eliza Anna Grier, the first black woman licensed to practice medicine in Georgia, hung out her shingle as an OB-GYN first in Atlanta, then in Greenville, South Carolina, and finally back in Georgia, in Thomasville.

Once again money was tight. In 1901 she reached out to women's rights activist Susan B. Anthony for help. Grier, thirty-seven, told Anthony that most of her patients were poor people and she, herself, had been quite ill for several weeks with "La Grippe" (influenza) and unable "to make a single dollar." What's more, there were "a great many forces" at work to keep black people from succeeding in business. "Please help me in this my time of severe trial & want," Dr. Grier pleaded.

Anthony, in her eighties, forwarded Dr. Grier's letter to WMCP. "Cannot you suggest to the girl some way out of her trouble?" she asked. The result of that letter is unknown, but about a year later Dr. Grier was dead, following a stroke.

In addition to the two previous women discussed—Rebecca Cole, who attended the school when it was the Female Medical College of Pennsylvania, and Halle Tanner Dillon Johnson—as well as Eliza Anna Grier, the Woman's Medical College of Pennsylvania (founded in 1850 and the world's second med school for women) produced several other outstanding black women physicians in the nineteenth century.

WMCP's doors were open to other women of color. There was Susan LaFlesche Picotte (class of 1889), for example: the first Native American MD. Too, WMCP admitted Jewish students at a time when many med schools in America did not.

WMCP evolved into the coed Medical College of Pennsylvania. In 2002 that school was folded into the Drexel University College of Medicine.

▲ **UNFLINCHING:** Woman's Medical College of Pennsylvania anatomy lab in circa 1892.

MARY ELIZA MAHONEY

1845–1926 • Nurse

FIRST

⁎ US black graduate of a nursing school (1879).

LEGACY

⁎ Spent much of her illustrious nursing career as a private-duty nurse, mostly for wealthy white people.

▲ **A FLORENCE NIGHTINGALE:** Boston-born Mary Eliza Mahoney in 1879.

BACKSTORY

⁎ Sixteen-month course at the all-woman-staffed New England Hospital for Women and Children in Boston (today's Dimock Community Health Center), one of America's first institutions to offer professional training in nursing (beginning in 1872).

⁎ Of the forty-two women who started the hospital's nurses' training course in 1878, only she and three other students completed it in 1879.

⁎ Before her formal training, she worked at the hospital for more than a dozen years—cleaner, laundress, cook, nurse's aide.

SARAH E. GOODE

1855–1905 • Inventor

A FOREMOTHER OF INVENTION

✳ There was no tiny-house movement in the days of Chicago's Sarah E. Goode. Yet many Americans did live in small homes and apartments. Goode—whose father was a carpenter and whose husband, Archibald, was identified on the 1880 US federal census as a "stair builder"—invented a contraption for cramped dwellings: a desk that doubled as a place to get some z's. For her forerunner of the hideaway bed Goode received a US patent—one of the first black women to do so—on July 14, 1885.

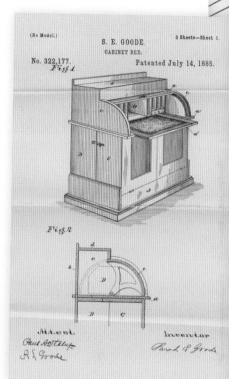

(No Model.)

S. E. GOODE.
CABINET BED.

No. 322,177.   Patented July 14, 1885.

3 Sheets—Sheet 1.

Fig 1

Fig. 2

Attest
Paul A. Staley
R. S. Goode

Inventor
Sarah E. Goode

▲ **INNOVATION:** One piece of the paperwork that accompanied Sarah E. Goode's patent application.

In 2012 the Sarah E. Goode STEM Academy opened at 7651 S. Holman Avenue in Chicago, Illinois.

JOSEPHINE SILONE YATES

1859–1912 • Science Educator

FIRST

* US black woman to head a college science department (c. June 1886–1889). This was at today's Lincoln University in Jefferson City, Missouri, founded by black soldiers after the Civil War. Yates began teaching there (botany, chemistry, physiology, and more) in 1881.

BACKSTORY

* Valedictorian in 1877 at Rogers High School in Newport, Rhode Island, where she graduated in three years instead of the usual four and where she was the school's first black student—and where she became keen on chemistry.

* Graduated with honors from the Rhode Island State Normal School in Providence (1879), after which she passed the teaching certification exam with flying colors and became the first black person certified to teach in Rhode Island's public school system.

"The aim of all true education is to give to body and soul all the beauty, strength, and perfection of which they are capable, to fit the individual for complete living."

—JOSEPHINE SILONE YATES

▲ **IN PURSUIT OF EXCELLENCE:** Josephine Silone Yates circa 1885. She was born in Mattituck, Long Island, to a native New Yorker (mother) and a Jamaican (father).

IDA GRAY NELSON ROLLINS

c. 1865–1953 • Doctor of Dental Surgery

FIRST

✳ US black woman doctor of dental surgery.

LEGACY

✳ Practiced for more than thirty years, first in Cincinnati, Ohio, then in Chicago, Illinois. Ida, said one source, "served all races, all ages, and both sexes" and was "considered especially good with children."

BACKSTORY

✳ Born in Clarksville, Tennessee, Ida was the daughter of a white man who apparently had nothing to do with her and a teen who died when her daughter was a baby. An aunt adopted Ida and soon after moved her with the rest of her family to Cincinnati.

In 1900, ten years after Ida became a Doctor of Dental Surgery, of America's 29,665 dentists 807 were women.

✳ In high school Ida worked for the dental practice of two white brothers: William and Jonathan Taft. The latter, a cofounder of the American Dental Association (1859) and dean of the dental school at the University of Michigan in Ann

Arbor, encouraged Ida to pursue dentistry. After three years of training at the Taft brothers' practice, Ida took the school's entrance exam.

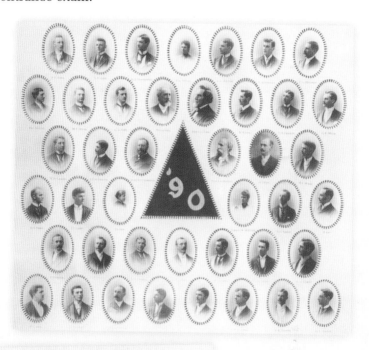

STUDENT'S RECORD.

DENTAL DEPARTMENT, UNIVERSITY OF MICHIGAN.

5. Osteology	C	5½	Dentistry, Operative	e
5. Practical Anatomy	C	5½	" Clinical	e
5. General Anatomy	e	5.	" Prosthetic	C
5. Histology	e	5½	Oral Surgery	e
4½ Physiology	e		Dental Anatomy	
4 5/2 General Chemistry	e			
5. Analytical Chemistry	e			

Name _Miss Ida Gray_
Residence _Cincinnati, O._
Age _____ Entered _October 1st_ 1887
Admitted on _Examination_
Preceptor _D. J. Taft_
Previous Study _Three Years_
Class _Freshman 3 yr._

ATTENDANCE.

1st year _39_ weeks. 2d year _____ weeks. 3d year _____ weeks.
STANDING: C, Completed. P. C., Partially completed. X, Exempt.

◄▲ **BRAVE:** Fourth row, third from the left, is Ida Gray Nelson Rollins in a photo composite of the University of Michigan College of Dentistry's Class of 1890. Also her report card from year one (1887). In 1997 the school established an award in Ida's honor.

ALICE AUGUSTA BALL

1892–1916 • Pharmaceutical Chemist

After earning *two* bachelor's degrees from the University of Washington in Seattle (in chemistry in 1912, in pharmacy in 1914), Alice was the first black person and first woman to earn a master's degree in science (chemistry) from the College of Hawai'i on the island of O'ahu. Her thesis: *The Chemical Constituents of Piper Methysticum or The Chemical Constituents of the Active Principle of the Ava Root.*

Yes, a mouthful! What it boils down to is Alice found a way to separate out—to extract—the active ingredient of the root of the ava—aka *awa* and *kava*—a shrub indigenous to the Pacific islands. For centuries people used this root in various forms as a sedative and pain killer. Alice sought to make the ava root a more powerful source of pain relief.

When J. F. Illingworth, head of the college's committee on advanced degrees, approved Alice's forty-four-page thesis in the spring of 1915, he stated

▲ **BRAINPOWER:** Seattle native Alice Ball in the University of Washington's 1911–1912 yearbook, *The Tyee.*

28

that it "clearly demonstrates her ability to do original work and to present her results in logical form." Someone else was also impressed with Alice's work: Dr. Harry T. Hollmann at Honolulu's Kalihi Hospital, which treated people with Hansen's disease, commonly called leprosy.

Hansen's disease is a bacteria-borne illness that can result in awful sores, the loss of fingers and toes, and blindness, among other things. Because there was no cure and the disease was thought to be highly contagious, its sufferers, called lepers since ancient times, were despised and often forced against their will to live in colonies. Hawai'i's leper colony was in Kalaupapa, on the island of Moloka'i, about twenty-five miles east of O'ahu.

In Alice's day the main treatment for Hansen's disease was an oil made from the seeds of the chaulmoogra tree, a

Alice lived in Honolulu briefly as a child after her parents, Laura Louise Ball (photographer and hairdresser) and James Presley Ball Jr. (attorney and photographer), decided to leave Seattle and accompany Grandpa Ball to Hawai'i. Grandpa Ball was James Presley Ball Sr., famed photographer, known professionally as J. P. Ball. And Grandpa suffered agonizing arthritis. The family hoped that a tropical clime would bring relief. After Grandpa Ball died in 1904, Alice and her parents returned to Seattle.

Alice's childhood days in Hawai'i may explain why, when it came to college, she said no to a scholarship from the University of California, Berkeley, and ae—Hawaiian for "yes"—to one from the College of Hawai'i. Grandpa Ball's arthritis may have inspired her research on the awa root.

tropical evergreen. This oil was applied to the skin, given orally, or injected. Results were hit-and-miss. Side effects could be horrendous. When it was taken by mouth, some patients experienced awful nausea. Injections sometimes left patients with blistered, burning skin, because the oil was insoluble and so wasn't readily absorbed by tissues in the body.

But what if the active ingredients of chaulmoogra oil could be separated out? wondered Dr. Hollman. *What if someone could come up with a water-soluble extract—one that would absorb into the skin?* Thinking of her success in extracting the active element of the ava, Dr. Hollmann turned to Alice Ball for help in extracting properties from another plant.

Alice, by then the first woman and first black chemistry instructor at the College of Hawai'i (now the University of Hawai'i), worked fast and furious on the chaulmoogra oil problem. By late 1915 or early 1916—problem solved! Alice came up with a water-soluble extract of the chaulmoogra oil. Injections wouldn't result in horrible side effects.

Until viable antibiotics were developed in the 1940s, Alice Ball's breakthrough was the basis for the number one treatment for people with Hansen's disease—a godsend for millions of children and adults.

The brilliant Alice Augusta Ball didn't live to see the wonder of her work. She died on New Year's Eve 1916 at age twenty-four. An early report stated that her death stemmed from overexposure to chlorine gas during a class demonstration.

After Alice's death, the College of Hawai'i's president, Arthur L. Dean, published an article on her discovery without giving her any credit. He called it "Dean's Method." In 1922 Dr. Hollmann tried to set the record straight in an article on Alice's leprosy-combatting work. He called it "Ball's Method." Still Alice's contribution to science languished in darkness, in shadows for years, until . . .

On February 29, 2000, the University of Hawai'i placed a bronze plaque in Alice's honor on its only existing chaulmoogra tree. Seven years later its Board of Regents posthumously gave Alice Augusta Ball the university's highest award: the Regents Medal of Distinction.

ANNA LOUISE JAMES

1886–1977 • Pharmacist

Home at 6 Winter Street in Hartford, Connecticut, became unbearable!

Tired of the way Stepmother had Daddy wrapped around her little finger . . .

Fed up with waiting on Stepmother hand and foot . . .

In 1902, sixteen-year-old Anna Louise James (Louise to family) ran away from home. She made a beeline for Old Saybrook, Connecticut, a mostly white village about a three-hour train ride away.

Louise fled to an enterprising couple: big sister **Bertha Lane**—chiropodist (a foot doctor), hairdresser, and linen-and-lace maker—and Bertha's husband, Peter Lane, one of Connecticut's first licensed black pharmacists. The couple ran Lane's Drugstore out of a two-story house at the corner of Main Street and Pennywise Lane, a house to which they had added a wing for an ice cream parlor. Living quarters were behind and above the shop. The Lanes had no children when Louise arrived but would soon have two daughters: Helen (1906) and Anna (1908).

While living with the Lanes, Anna Louise James, having ditched school in Hartford, earned her diploma from Saybrook High at age nineteen.

Along the way, too . . .

Tinctures and tablets, pills and potions, patent medicines

and prescriptions, balms and cobalt blue medicine bottles—being around all that . . .

In 1906, with financial help from the Lanes, Louise went where no black woman had ever gone before: to the Brooklyn (New York) College of Pharmacy on Nostrand Avenue. This school's first black female student was the only woman among more than fifty students in the class of 1908.

"Anna L. James having completed the courses of study and training in . . ." That's how her diploma begins. Those courses and that training included chemistry, botany, pharmacognosy, toxicology, and *materia medica*. While studying her brains out, Louise had also served as class secretary.

The Greek **pharmakon** (φάρμακον), meaning "drug" + the Greek **gnosis** (γνῶσις), meaning "knowledge" = Phar-ma-cog-nosy, the study of drugs derived from nature's creations. *Materia medica* is Latin for "medical materials," or knowledge of the healing properties of curatives.

One of Connecticut's first female licensed pharmacists, Louise went into business in Hartford, at 141 Mathers Street. In a 1915 speech at a black business league's convention in Boston, she spoke of the long hours she put in. She stated that "in the five years of my business experience, I have had twenty-five days vacation, including holidays. I find that I must be at my post each day if I would succeed."

Louise's post soon changed. Back in Old Saybrook she

▲ **DROPOUT TO DRUGGIST:** Anna Louise James in the early 1900s.

became a partner in Lane's Drugstore. Then, when big sis and brother-in-law moved to Hartford, Louise became sole proprietor, renaming the shop James' Pharmacy. Added to that, she opened another drugstore a few miles away in Old Lyme, a shop her brother Fritz managed. Years later Louise's niece **Anna Lane**, a graduate of the Connecticut College of Pharmacy, worked in both shops—but not forever. After Anna, who at some point dropped the last "a" from her name, married writer George David Petry in 1938, and the couple moved to New York City. There Ann Petry pursued a passion that trumped dispensing pills and potions: writing. Her 1946 novel, *The Street*, was the first novel by a black woman to sell more than a million copies. Her first children's book, *The Drug Store Cat* (1949), stars Buzzie, a frisky feline sent to live with a brother and sister who own a pharmacy, Mr. and Miss James.

Louise's alma mater, the Brooklyn College of Pharmacy, is today's Long Island University's Arnold & Marie Schwartz College of Pharmacy and Health Sciences.

PART 2

Riding the Wave

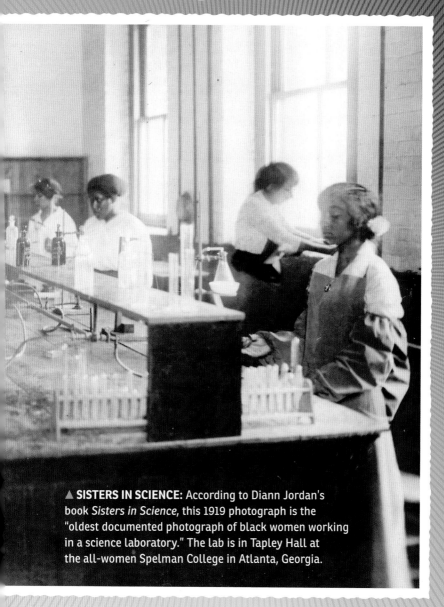

▲ **SISTERS IN SCIENCE:** According to Diann Jordan's book *Sisters in Science*, this 1919 photograph is the "oldest documented photograph of black women working in a science laboratory." The lab is in Tapley Hall at the all-women Spelman College in Atlanta, Georgia.

First Wave Feminism started in the nineteenth century. A milestone moment came in July 1848: a two-day convention on women's rights in Seneca Falls, New York, an event spearheaded by two white women, Elizabeth Cady Stanton and Lucretia Mott. The roughly three hundred attendees included Frederick Douglass and about forty other men.

The Seneca Falls convention's shining achievement was the Declaration of Sentiments. Modeled after the Declaration of Independence, it was a cri de coeur for women to have equality of opportunity in education, employment, and in other arenas. It also called for women to have the right to vote nationwide.

That didn't happen until August 18, 1920, when the Nineteenth Amendment to the US Constitution was ratified. (Black and other male citizens of color had gained the right to the national vote in 1870 through the Fifteenth Amendment, but neither male nor female Washington, DC, residents could vote for president until 1961—and they still had no representation in Congress.)

After the Nineteenth Amendment, more women, along with some men, stepped up their campaign for folks to chuck antiquated notions of what women can do.

As hemlines rose, as more women got behind the wheels of cars, as jazz became the rage, more US black women geared up for a life in STEM.

WILLA BEATRICE BROWN

1906–1992 • Aviator

Enoch P. Waters remembered this: "When Willa Brown, a shapely young brownskin woman, wearing white jodhpurs, a form fitting white jacket and white boots, strode into our newsroom, in 1936, she made such a stunning appearance that all the typewriters suddenly went silent."

▲ **HIGHFLYER**: Willa Beatrice Brown (date unknown), born in Glasgow, Kentucky, and raised mostly in Terre Haute, Indiana. Brown's great inspiration was **Bessie Coleman**, the first US black woman licensed pilot. Unable to find a flight school in the States that would admit her, Coleman earned her wings in France (1921).

The newsroom into which bold Willa strode was that of the *Chicago Defender*, a leading black-owned weekly. Waters was its city editor.

"Unlike most first time visitors," he continued, Willa "wasn't at all bewildered. She had a confident bearing and there was an undercurrent of determination in her husky voice as she announced, not asked, that she wanted to see me."

Willa was on a mission to get the *Defender* to cover an upcoming air show by the Challenger Air Pilots Association, Chicago's first black flying club. One of the club's cofounders was Cornelius Coffey, ace aviation mechanic and flight instructor at Harlem Airport in southwest Chicago, site of that upcoming air show.

Cornelius Coffey, to whom Willa would be married briefly, was one of the men who taught her to fly, a skill that requires not only nerves of steel but also some serious math skills. For calculating descents in different types of weather, for example. Or for determining the amount of fuel needed to get from point A to point B.

Back to Willa B. Brown and Enoch P. Waters.

Willa got her way. Enoch P. Waters covered the air show himself. He even climbed aboard a Piper Club with her, despite the fact that it struck him as "a rather frail craft."

Up! Up! Up! In that Piper Cub (most likely yellow and definitely lightweight)—Waters found it "a thrilling experience and the maneuvers, figure eights, flip overs and stalls, were exhilarating though, momentarily, frightening."

The *Defender,* along with other black-owned newspapers, gave quite a bit of ink to Willa's rise in aviation.

"YOUNG WOMAN FLYER GETS PILOT'S LICENSE" began a headline in the July 2, 1938, *Pittsburgh Courier.* Willa had made history as the first black woman to earn a private pilot's license in the States. This was a few months after she had earned her solo license.

Of the fifteen people who took the test for a private pilot's license at Chicago's Curtiss Field airstrip in the summer of 1938, Willa was the only black person and the only woman. And, noted the *Courier,* "Miss Brown passed her examinations with the highest mark, 96, of the entire class." What's more, while only forty hours of flying were required for a private pilot's license, Willa had clocked nearly a hundred before taking that written exam. And not only could she fly a plane, Willa could fix one, too. She had a master mechanic's certificate from Chicago's Curtiss-Wright Aeronautical University.

With a private pilot's license Willa could take people up for a spin and give flying lessons. But she wanted to spread her wings. "I shall work next fall toward getting a limited commercial license," she told a reporter. "That will permit me to take up passengers for pay." Before 1939 was out, Willa had that commercial license.

That same year Willa cofounded the National Airmen Association of America, intent on beefing up the number of black aviation enthusiasts. A year later she helped get the Chicago Girls Flight Club off the ground as well as the Coffey

School of Aeronautics. (Willa was eminently qualified to run things. Back in 1927 she had earned a bachelor's degree in business from Indiana State Teachers College and in 1937 a master's degree in business administration from Chicago's Northwestern University.)

When the Coffey School of Aeronautics opened, World War II was raging in Europe, and America's entry was on the horizon. More than a few of the black men who trained at Willa's school became Tuskegee Airmen, the first black flyboys in the US Army Air Corps (predecessor of the US Air Force).

During World War II roughly 350,000 women served in the US armed forces. They were WACs (members of the Women's Army Corps, originally the Women's Army Auxiliary Corps known as WAACs), WASPs (Women's Air Force Service Pilots), WAVES (the Navy's Women Accepted for Volunteer Emergency Service), and SPARs (the Coast Guard's Women's Reserve—derived from the Coast Guard's Latin motto *Semper Paratus*, meaning "Always Ready"). WACs, WASPs, WAVES, and SPARs did a range of work, clerical to medical, that freed up men to fight.

During the war, troops of women also entered the civilian workforce for the first time. They worked in munitions factories, built ships, drove taxis and ambulances, took to the bandstands, pumped gas. Sadly, after the war, many were sacked and their jobs given to returning fighters.

The old propaganda was back: A woman's place is in the home and in traditional women's work.

A host of women said, *Oh no!*, giving rise to the second wave of feminism.

Willa also contributed to the war effort. In 1942 she became the first black female officer in the Civil Air Patrol (CAP). This government agency conducted border patrols, provided courier services, and in other ways helped out the US Army Air Corps on the home front.

RUTH ELLA MOORE

1903–1994 • Bacteriologist

FIRST

✶ US black woman to earn a PhD in a natural science.

LEGACY

✶ In graduate school she researched tuberculosis, still a leading cause of death worldwide.

✶ As a professor at Howard University Medical College in Washington, DC, she researched such nasties as the largely food-borne bacteria *Salmonella* and *E. coli* that still wreak havoc today.

BACKSTORY

✶ Bachelor of science degree (1926) from Ohio State University (OSU) in Columbus, Ohio, where she was born.

✶ Master of science degree (1927) from OSU.

✶ PhD (1933) in bacteriology from OSU.

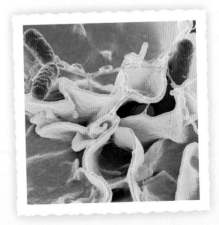

▶ **YUCK!:** This photograph (color-enhanced) shows the bacteria *Salmonella* (red) invading human cells. The intestinal tract infection salmonellosis can, among other things, result in intense stomach pain, fever, and chills.

MARTHA EUPHEMIA LOFTON HAYNES

1890–1980 • Mathematician

FIRST

✳ US black woman to earn a PhD in mathematics— and accomplished at age fifty-three!

LEGACY

✳ Distinguished Washington, DC, teacher for more than fifty years (who put teaching on hold while working on that PhD).

▲ **PROBLEM SOLVER:** Martha Euphemia Lofton Haynes as a young woman

✳ Retired in 1959 as head of the mathematics department at today's University of the District of Columbia.

BACKSTORY

✳ Bachelor's degree in mathematics with a minor in psychology (1914) from the women's college Smith, in Northampton, Massachusetts.

✳ Master's degree in education (1930) from the University of Chicago.

✳ PhD in mathematics (1943) from the Catholic University of America in DC, where she was born and raised.

ALFREDA JOHNSON WEBB

1923–1992 • Doctor of Veterinary Medicine

* * * * *

JANE HINTON

1919–2003 • Doctor of Veterinary Medicine

TIED FOR FIRST: DVMS

* In 1949 two US black women earned DVMs (Doctor of Veterinary Medicine) for the first time.

Alfreda Johnson Webb, a native of Mobile, Alabama, got her DVM from Tuskegee Institute (now University) in Tuskegee, Alabama, where she had earned a bachelor of science. Tuskegee's school of veterinary medicine, the only one at a historically black college or university, was established in 1945, and Alfreda was the only woman in its class of 1949. After Tuskegee, Dr. Webb went to school yet again: to Michigan State in East Lansing for a master's in anatomy (1951). Next she enjoyed an illustrious teaching career at Tuskegee, then at North Carolina Agricultural & Technical State College (now University) in Greensboro.

Jane Hinton, born in Canton, Massachusetts, earned her DVM from the University of Pennsylvania School of Veterinary Medicine. After that she ran a small-animal clinic in Framingham, Massachusetts, then became a livestock inspector for the federal government.

Humans also benefited from Dr. Hinton's scientific mind. Back in 1941, while working as a lab tech at Harvard, she and colleague John Howard Mueller developed an ideal formula for agar, a brown, jelly-like substance used to test the effectiveness of antibiotics against gonorrhea (a sexually transmitted disease) and meningitis (a deadly brain inflammation). Labs the world over have used the Mueller-Hinton Agar (MHA) to determine the most effective drugs to treat or eliminate other diseases.

Jane's father was a major influence on her pursuit of a life in science. He was bacteriologist and pathologist William Augustus Hinton, Harvard University's first black professor.

▲ **CATS AND DOGS AND MORE:** The Latin *veterinarius* = related or having to do with beasts of burden.

GEORGIA LOUISE HARRIS BROWN

1918–1999 • Architect

As a kid Georgia Louise loved to draw, paint, tinker with mechanical things.

When this native of Topeka, Kansas, grew up, she maximized her aptitude—for algebra, trigonometry, calculus, physics (and more!)—and her adeptness—with T-squares, triangles, compasses (and more!)—to become the second US black woman licensed architect. She, who went by Louise for much of life, achieved this in 1949, seven years after Chicagoan **Beverly Loraine Greene** became the first.

In the summer of 1938, with two years of college under her belt (Topeka's Washburn University), Louise visited a brother in Chicago. While there, she took courses at the Armour Institute of Technology. She later studied architecture at the Illinois Institute of Technology (IIT, a merger of the Armour Institute and the Lewis Institute). Still later, after kicking it back to Kansas, Louise became the first black woman to earn a bachelor's degree in architecture from the University of Kansas in Lawrence. This was in 1944.

Louise returned to Chicago. There, one mentor was Kenneth Roderick O'Neal, a black architect and structural engineer for whom she worked from 1945 to 1949. Another mentor was the German American architect Ludwig Mies van der Rohe, with whom she had studied at Armour and at IIT. Mies was in the forefront of modernist architecture.

▶ **T-SQUARES, SLIDE RULES, PROTRACTORS—AND BOWS, TOO:** Georgia Louise Harris Brown in the December 3, 1949, *Pittsburgh Courier*. She was soon behind a drafting board at Frank J. Kornacker & Associates, Inc., a white-owned structural engineering firm in Chicago, where she was its only licensed woman architect. While holding down this day job, Georgia took night courses in civil engineering at IIT's Institute of Design (1950–1953). **Anat Falbel** (civil engineer and architectural historian) and **Roberta Washington** (one of the first US black women to have her own architectural firm, established in 1983), discovered that at the Institute, Georgia "excelled in ten subjects." They included calculus I, calculus II, concrete and foundation design, differential equations, mechanics of materials, and soil mechanics.

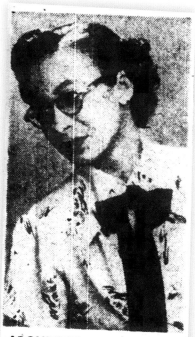

ARCHITECT — Petite Mrs. Louise Harris-Brown of Chicago holds the distinction of being the second Negro woman licensed achitect in the United States. Mrs. Brown, who is a graduate of the University of Kansas, works for K. Roderick O'Neal, outstanding Chicago architect. She describes her most exciting experience as working on reinforced concrete and multi-storyed apartment buildings designed by the famous Mies Van der Rohe.— —ANP.

Out with excessive ornamentation and clutter!

Onward to open floor plans and boldness with simplicity!

Louise did structural calculations for two Mies master-piece apartment buildings in Chicago: the Promontory Apartments in Hyde Park and 860–880 Lake Shore Drive in the Streeterville section of the city.

In the fall of 1953, with studies of Portuguese under her belt, Louise packed her bags and moved to Brazil. There, for several years she worked at Charles Bosworth's São Paulo firm, which specialized in industrial projects. In 1970, the year she was licensed in Brazil, Louise launched the construction company Brown Bottene with the couple Neyde Bottene Camacho and Petronio Theodoro Camacho. After it closed, in 1976 Louise launched the architectural firm Gryphus with engineer Anibal de Almeida Fernandes. This firm was in operations until 1993, when Louise returned to the States due to illness.

During her nearly forty years in Brazil Georgia Louise Harris Brown designed and oversaw the construction of homes for Brazilian VIPs as well as that of offices and plants for Kodak, Ford Motor Company, and other US companies.

The Greek **arkhi** (ἀρχι) meaning "chief" or "principal" + **téktōn** (τέκτων) meaning "builder" = architect (master builder)

ANGIE LENA TURNER KING

1905–2004 • Mathematician & Chemist

This native of Elkhorn, a small West Virginia coal-mining town, once told an interviewer, "I had it tough, but it hasn't bothered my mind."

Tough is being eight years old when your mother dies.

Tough is being separated for a time from your father, little sister, and big brother.

Tough is being dark skinned and living with a very light-skinned grandmother who despises your color, who calls you the "black b——" (rhymes with witch).

Despite tough times, in 1919 Angie graduated from high school at age *fourteen.*

On she went to Bluefield Colored Institute (now Bluefield State College) to equip herself to be a teacher.

On she went to West Virginia Collegiate Institute, a few miles outside Charleston (established in 1890 as the West Virginia Colored Institute).

Going on and on was *tough!* Angie was her own sole source of financial support. She washed dishes, waited tables—"anything like that I could get."

Toughing it out, Annie graduated from the institute with honors in 1927. With her bachelor's degree in mathematics and chemistry, she began teaching at the institute's high school.

And Angie kept on going.

She spent summers in Ithaca, New York, earning a master's degree in mathematics and chemistry from Cornell University. She accomplished this in 1931—two years into the Great Depression when hard economic times forced many people to drop out of school and left legions of Americans jobless, even homeless.

After eight years as a high school teacher, Angie became an associate professor of mathematics and chemistry at her alma mater, by then renamed West Virginia State College (now University). There Angie was a beacon light for scores of students. She toughened their mental muscle, spurred them on to higher heights. One of her mentees was math prodigy **Katherine Johnson**, who became a household name after the release of the book and later the movie *Hidden Figures*. Katherine Johnson, class of 1937, remembered King as "a wonderful teacher—bright, caring, and very rigorous."

Years after Johnson graduated from West Virginia State,

▲ **A BEAUTIFUL MIND:**
Dr. Angie Lena Turner King in the 1971 West Virginia State University yearbook, *The Arch.* Dr. King retired from teaching in 1980.

her wonderful, rigorous mentor went back to school yet again. Angie Lena Turner King—professor *and* wife *and* mother— earned a PhD in mathematics and chemistry in 1955 from the University of Pittsburgh, today about a three-hour drive from Institute, West Virginia.

Dr. Angie was truly one tough lady.

Greek **mathēmatikós** (μαθηματικός) = "fond of learning."

MYRA ADELE LOGAN

1908–1977 • Medical Doctor, Surgeon & Researcher

FIRST

* Woman and ninth person to perform open heart surgery (1943), fifty years after a black man, Dr. Daniel Hale Williams with Chicago's Provident Hospital, performed the first.

* Black woman member of the American College of Surgeons (1951), which admits only surgeons of the highest caliber.

LEGACY

* Cofounded in 1945 one of the first group practices: Harlem's Upper Manhattan Group. "We practice together because no one doctor knows everything," she told New York's *Daily News* in the summer of 1964. "It's easier and better to have a lab and a radiologist right downstairs, or a pediatrician next door." The Upper Manhattan Group then consisted of twenty-six doctors and owned a building at 152nd Street and Amsterdam Avenue.

* Member of a 1960s team of physicians that developed an X-ray technique that led to earlier detection of breast cancer.

BACKSTORY

* Native of Tuskegee, Alabama, who graduated valedictorian with a bachelor of arts degree (1927) from Atlanta University (now Clark-Atlanta University).

* Master's degree in psychology (1928) from Columbia University.

▶ **CALLING DOCTOR MYRA ADELE LOGAN:** *Left to right:* Drs. Lyndon M. Hill, Louis T. Wright (whose two daughters were physicians), Myra Adele Logan, and Aaron Prigot with an unidentified patient and a Harlem Hospital employee. Date unknown.

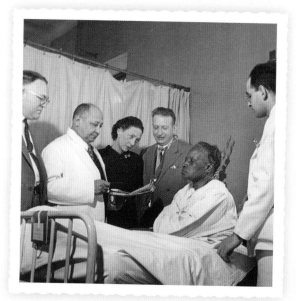

✳ First recipient (1929) of the recently established Walter Gray Crump scholarship: a $10,000 award exclusively for black men and women who wanted to study medicine. Mr. Crump, a white surgeon, was the son of abolitionist Samuel Crump.

✳ MD (1933) from the then New York Homeopathic Medical College and Flower Hospital in New York City (now part of the Touro College and University System in Valhalla, New York).

✳ Married to acclaimed artist Charles Alston. In 1940 he created two murals for Harlem Hospital: *Magic in Medicine* and *Modern Medicine* (both still in exsistence!). Myra was a model for a portrait in *Modern Medicine*.

FLEMMIE KITTRELL

1904–1980 • Home Economist

Young Flemmie cried when promoted to second grade. Moving on meant leaving a teacher she adored. "She was really that teacher who gave me my great love for school," said Flemmie years later.

A whiz when it came to schoolwork, as she herself admitted, Flemmie "was not too alert when it came to working on the farm." That farm was her family's place in Henderson, North Carolina.

When Flemmie was a child, many farmers' children didn't even finish grammar school because the land needed their labor. But Flemmie's parents didn't put the kibosh on her love for book learning. They let her proceed from grade to grade, then on to Hampton Academy, the preparatory school at Hampton Institute (now Hampton University) in Hampton, Virginia.

When Flemmie headed to Hampton, she had her family's blessings but not the funds needed for tuition and other expenses, so she worked her way through school.

As graduation loomed, Flemmie, keen on college, tossed and turned over what field of study to pursue.

History?

Political science?

Economics?

"But have you thought of home economics?" asked teacher Blanche Rollonson.

▲ **GLOBETROTTER:** Dr. Flemmie Kittrell in 1968, pointing out the nations where Cornell home economists had an impact.

"I don't think I'd like that."

"Why not?"

"I didn't have a good reason," said Flemmie years later, "except I thought the home was just so ordinary, women know all about it."

Think again, Rollonson essentially said. She urged Flemmie to read a biography of home economics pioneer Ellen H. Swallow Richards, a white chemist who in 1870 became the first woman admitted to a scientific school, the Massachusetts Institute of Technology (MIT) in Cambridge.

After Flemmie read that book on Richards, she was sold on home economics, aka home science, aka domestic science, the study of people—individuals, families, communities—and their environments with an eye on improving their quality of life.

At Hampton Institute Flemmie majored in home economics and later earned a PhD in the field—a first for a woman of color—from the New York State College of Home Economics at Cornell University in Ithaca, New York (1936).

Flemmie returned to Hampton in 1940 to head its home economics department. A few years later she was tapped to do the same at Howard University in Washington, DC.

At Howard, "Kittrell redesigned the program to include research into the real-life problems faced by families every day, especially low-income families that struggled to obtain nutritious meals and sanitary living conditions," wrote Charles W. Carey Jr. in *African Americans in Science.*

Flemmie Kittrell pioneered on another front when she established a nursery school at Howard. It became a model for Head Start: an initiative launched in 1965 to provide children from low-income families with educational and health services (including good nutrition).

By then Flemmie had traveled the world, often sponsored by the US State Department. In the late 1940s, for example, she took a leave of absence from Howard to spend six months in Liberia, West Africa. Her study of people's diets shone the spotlight on "hidden hunger": instances of children and adults with bellies full (of mostly starches) who are, in fact, malnourished because their diets lack sufficient proteins and fruits and vegetables.

In 1950 Flemmie made her first trip to India. This was at the behest of writer and reformer Hansa Jivraj Mehta, vice chancellor of the University of Baroda in the state of Gujarat. There Flemmie helped get India's first college of home economics off the ground—from developing its faculty to fashioning courses.

Bangladesh . . . Ghana . . . Japan . . . Morocco . . . Mozambique . . . the Netherlands . . . Nigeria . . . Zaire (now Congo) . . .

Flemmie, who saw herself as a citizen of the world, traveled to more than a dozen countries lecturing on and teaching home economics, a field she saw as a composite one, drawing on a range of disciplines, from biology and bacteriology to psychology, economics, and the fine arts.

As Wini Warren put it in *Black Women Scientists in the United States*, for Dr. Flemmie Kittrell, "home economics was the science of living."

"No country can go higher than the performance of its women. If women are kept down, the men will keep themselves down. When one educates a man, one educates an individual; when one educates a girl, one educates a whole family." —FLEMMIE KITTRELL

CAROLYN BEATRICE PARKER

1917–1966 • Physicist

▲ **AN ALMOST PhD:**
Carolyn Beatrice Parker in 1949.

In the 1940s, during World War II, this native of Gainesville, Florida, worked on a top-secret research project: the Dayton Project.

At a military base in Ohio, protected by armed guards and barbed wire, Carolyn Parker and other scientists conducted research on polonium, a very rare, very radioactive metal. The Dayton Project was part of America's larger (and equally hush-hush) Manhattan Project: the research and development of the first atomic bomb, and polonium was needed for detonation.

Parker's qualifications included a bachelor's degree in physics (*magna cum laude*) from Fisk University, in Nashville, Tennessee (1936), and a master's degree in mathematics from the University of Michigan (1941).

A few years after her work on the Dayton Project, in 1951 Carolyn earned a second master's degree, this one in physics, from the world-famous Massachusetts Institute of Technology (MIT) in Cambridge. She was on track to become the first US black woman to earn a PhD in physics (from MIT) when leukemia struck. Caused possibly by exposure to polonium while on the Dayton Project, it eventually took Carolyn Beatrice Parker's life.

Physics, the study of matter and energy and what happens when they mix—or collide—comes from the Greek **physikos** (φύσηκος), meaning "natural."

MARIE MAYNARD DALY

1921–2003 • Biochemist

Where Dad was not able to succeed, daughter did.

As a child growing up in Corona, Queens, New York, Marie knew of her father's dream deferred. As a young man he, Ivan Daly, had his heart set on studying chemistry at Cornell University in Ithaca, New York. While Ivan Daly did get a scholarship to attend Cornell, he wasn't able to come up with the additional money needed for all his expenses. He left after one semester and eventually became a postal worker in New York City.

▲ **LOOKING FORWARD:** Marie Maynard Daly in 1942, the year she graduated from Queens College.

Marie, the oldest of her parents' three children, inherited her father's love for science. She devoured books such as Paul De Kruif's classic *Microbe Hunters*. After excelling at one of New York City's finest public schools, the then all-girl Hunter College High School in Manhattan, Marie went to Queens College, from which she graduated *magna cum laude* with a bachelor's degree in chemistry in 1942.

Next up: New York University, where she earned a master's degree in chemistry.

Next up: Columbia University, where she became the first US black woman to earn a PhD in chemistry in 1947.

Next up?

Dr. Daly taught physical science at Howard University in Washington, DC, having been hired by black physicist Herman Branson. With esteemed white chemist Linus C. Pauling, Branson worked on the chemical structure of Hgb: hemoglobin, a protein in red blood cells that transports oxygen throughout the body. In the process Branson hit upon the cause of sickle cell anemia, a condition that mostly afflicts people of African descent.

While at Howard, Daly was eager to hear back from the American Cancer Society about a grant that would allow her to work for a year at Manhattan's Rockefeller Institute for Medical Research (now Rockefeller University). Daly was keen to join the research team headed by the school's biochemist Alfred Ezra Mirsky.

In 1988 Dr. Daly established a merit-based scholarship for students majoring in the physical sciences at Queens College. Originally she named it after her father, but later she added her mother's name for the making of the Ivan C. and Helen H. Daly Scholarship.

Dr. Daly got her wish. What's more, when her year at the Rockefeller Institute was up, she was kept on as a paid researcher. While working with Mirsky, Daly conducted research on cell and molecular biology, studying what was going on inside of cells and how they were involved in protein synthesis, that is, creating proteins that are essential for life. This was a time of intense research on both RNA (ribonucleic acid), a molecule in cells that is vital to new cell growth, and DNA (deoxyribonucleic acid), the genetic map or "blueprint" of who you are.

▲ **THE TWISTED LADDER:** In 1962, scientists Francis Crick (British), James Watson (American), and Maurice Wilkins (British) received a Nobel Prize in Physiology or Medicine for their 1953 discovery that DNA molecules form a double helix: two threadlike strands of nucleotides (RNA and DNA building blocks). The discovery paved the way for today's biotechnology. The three white men's Noble Prize for the discovery of this twisted ladder galls many people today, because other scientists deserved credit, too, most notably the white British chemist Rosalind Franklin. Speaking of credit: In James Watson's printed Nobel Prize speech, he acknowledged the research of Marie Maynard Daly along with that of some seventy other scientists.

Daly continued on strong as a biochemist, and in 1955 she went to Columbia University's College of Physicians and Surgeons where she began some of her most important work: a matter of the heart. She was determined to find the link between high cholesterol and clogged arteries, believed to be one cause of heart attacks. In 1960 Dr. Daly became a professor at the Albert Einstein College of Medicine of Yeshiva University in the Bronx, New York.

Dr. Daly's preeminent work lives on. Her research is still being used today to understand the cholesterol–heart attack connection.

In May 1993 the journal *Social Studies of Science* published science historian Margaret W. Rossiter's article "The ~~Matthew~~ Matilda Effect in Science" about the silence on and even suppression of women's contributions to science, with men often receiving credit for their work. Rossiter named this phenomenon in honor of Matilda Joslyn Gage, a white nineteenth-century American women's rights activist. This contributor to *The Woman's Bible*, coeditor of the multi-volume *History of the Woman Suffrage*, and author of the pamphlet *Woman as Inventor*, wrote Rossiter, "was aware of, and denounced, the tendency of men to prohibit women from reaping the fruits of their own toil, and in fact noticed that the more woman worked the more the men around her profited and the less credit she got." In coining the term "the Matilda Effect" Rossiter was counterpointing Robert K. Merton's 1968 "the Matthew Effect," often boiled down to mean "the rich get richer and the poor get poorer" (taken from Matthew 13:12 in the Bible).

JANE COOKE WRIGHT

1919–2013 • Oncologist

▲ **THE WRIGHT STUFF:** Jane Cooke Wright in 1962. Wonder what's in that little container? Me, too.

FIRST

✳ US black woman associate dean (along with professor of surgery and director of cancer research) at a major med school: her alma mater, New York Medical College (1967–75).

✳ Woman elected president of the New York Cancer Society (1971), cornerstone of the American Cancer Society.

LEGACY

✳ As a staffer and eventually director of Harlem Hospital's Cancer Research Foundation (CRF) 1949–1955, conducted research that advanced the more effective use of chemicals (chemotherapy developed in the 1940s) to destroy cancer cells. At the time leading treatments were surgery and radiation. For her work, in 1952 *Mademoiselle* magazine hailed this native New Yorker as one of America's ten "Young Women of the Year" and gave her its Merit Award.

✳ At New York University Medical Center, as associate professor of surgical research and head of research on chemotherapy (1955–1967), she was a pathfinder in precision medicine: Using biopsies (tissue samples) of tumors, she ran tests to come up with the best drugs for specific kinds of tumors.

✳ With six white men, cofounded in 1964 what is today the world's leading oncology organization: the American Society of Clinical Oncology, created to advance the use of clinical trials (tests on human beings) in researching chemotherapy. (That same year President Lyndon Johnson appointed Dr. Wright to the President's Commission on Heart Disease, Cancer, and Stroke.)

Greek **ónkos** (ὄγκος) meaning "lump or mass" + **logia**, a Latinization of the Greek **logos** (λόγος), meaning "the study of" = oncology.

BACKSTORY

✳ Bachelor of arts degree (1942) from Smith College in Northampton, Massachusetts.

✳ MD (1945) from New York Medical College with honors (and on full scholarship).

✳ Internship (training) and residencies (even more training) at New York City's Bellevue and Harlem hospitals (1945–1948).

✳ Medicine was a family affair. Her paternal grandfather, Ceah K. Wright, born into slavery, earned an MD in 1883 from one of America's first med schools for black people, Meharry, in Nashville, Tennessee. Her paternal step-grandfather, William Fletcher Penn, was the first black person to graduate from Yale Medical College in New Haven, Connecticut (1897), and his brother Dr. I. Garland Penn, journalist and educator, was a founder of the National Medical Association (1903), a networking and advocacy organization for black medical professionals established as the National Association of Colored Physicians, Dentists and Pharmacists in 1895. Jane Cooke Wright's uncle Harold Dadford West, biochemist, was Meharry Medical College's first black president (1952–1963). Her father, surgeon Louis Tompkins Wright, one of the first black graduates of Harvard Med (1915), established Harlem Hospital's CRF (1948). Her younger sister **Barbara Wright Pierce** became a specialist in occupational medicine: the branch of medicine that zeros in on accident and disease prevention and people's all-around health in the workplace. One of Jane Cooke Wright's daughters, **Jane Wright Jones,** became a psychiatrist; the other, **Alison Jones,** a clinical psychologist.

ANNIE EASLEY

1933–2011 • Mathematician & Computer Scientist

Math came easy for Annie when she was a kid growing up in Birmingham, Alabama, raised by a single mother. Many years later, while a homemaker in Cleveland, Ohio, this math whiz stumbled upon a newspaper article about twin sisters working as human computers at the city's Aircraft Engine Research Laboratory. The article said that this lab needed more women with mad math skills.

Hmm, thought Annie.

This was in 1955. The lab was a division of a federal agency, the National Advisory Committee for Aeronautics (NACA).

Within about two weeks of applying, Annie had a job there. And she didn't even have a college degree.

After high school Annie enrolled in Xavier University in New Orleans, Louisiana, where she intended to major in pharmacy. Annie said bye-bye to college after marriage to a serviceman led to a move to Cleveland, where his parents lived. So that's how Annie ended up one day at home reading an article about those twin sisters at a NACA lab, where with slide rules, clunky adding machines, and other tools, these human computers worked on complex computations for engineers.

On October 4, 1957, America's archenemy, the Soviet Union—a federation of communist countries, officially the Union of Soviet Socialist
Republics (USSR)—launched *Sputnik I*, the first successful artificial
satellite, a great leap forward in space exploration. About a month
later the Soviet Union launched *Sputnik II*.

America hated being bested. Thus the creation of NASA: to
enable the United States to catch up with, then overtake, the USSR
in the space race.

Sputnik I and *Sputnik II* also put the government on a mission
to beef up STEM brainpower among its youth.

In 1958, with the space race on—USA vs. USSR—NACA
was absorbed into the newly formed National Aeronautics and
Space Administration (NASA). The lab where Annie Easley
worked became the Lewis Research Center (now the Glenn
Research Center). And Annie kept on crunching numbers.

With the advent of electronic computers in the late 1950s,
human computers were no longer needed.

But programmers were.

Using the programming languages Fortran (Formula
Translation) and SOAP (Simple Object Access Protocol),
Annie did coding that enabled engineers to work out glitches
in the Centaur rocket: an upper-stage launch vehicle con-
ceived in the late 1950s and first used in 1966 to boost *Surveyor 1,* America's first unpiloted vehicle to land on the moon.
Its mission: to amass data about the lunar surface in prepa-
ration for NASA landing astronauts on the moon. Mission
accomplished with *Apollo 11* in 1969.

▲ **VERY CALCULATING:** Annie Easley in the central control room of the Engine Research Building at NASA's Lewis Research Center in Cleveland, Ohio. In this photo, which first appeared on the cover of the spring 1982 issue of NASA's *Science and Engineering Newsletter*, Easley is checking how much power facilities are using.

During her thirty-plus-year career at NASA—one that included work on wind-energy projects and storage batteries similar to those used in hybrid cars today—Annie Easley finally got a college degree by going to school at nights: a bachelor's degree in mathematics from Cleveland State University. Mission accomplished in 1977.

"My first bit of advice would be to get all of the math you can in junior and senior high school. Any math course that is offered, *take it!* Accept the challenge that it represents. Don't just blindly accept someone else's opinion who may say that math or science or some other academic course is too hard. If you will look around you, you'll find that you have a lot of role models. . . . You have a brain; you can use it. . . . Then, when you are ready for college, I want you to take college very seriously. It is not some kind of playground. It is the place where you can get the knowledge to take you out into the real world."

—ANNIE EASLEY, WHEN ASKED IN THE 1980S FOR
HER ADVICE TO YOUNG WOMEN, PARTICULARLY
YOUNG BLACK WOMEN, CONSIDERING A CAREER
IN MATHEMATICS.

YVONNE YOUNG CLARK

1929–2019 • Mechanical Engineer

I always liked to build things as a child," said Yvonne in a 1997 interview. "I had an Erector set and I fixed things around the house." Those things ranged from "the furnace stoker to the toaster," she recalled in an earlier interview for *US Black Engineer* magazine.

As a kid growing up in Louisville, Kentucky, this daughter of a surgeon (father) and librarian and journalist

▲ **IN GEAR:** Yvonne Young Clark, circa 1960–1969.

(mother) had her sights set on becoming an airplane pilot. She was bedazzled by talk of aeronautic exploits by black pilots operating at nearby Godman Army Airfield, guests at her parents' dinner parties. (A pilot or two took Yvonne up for a spin and let her work the controls. Also, as a girl "I was Annie Oakley," she said—a fine shot with a rifle and .45 pistol.)

For the love of flying, Yvonne took an aeronautics class

in high school, "where she built airplanes and crash-landed them from the fire escape at her high school," wrote Diann Jordan in her book *Sisters in Science*. And Yvonne was disappointed big-time when she couldn't take the mechanical drawing class. The teacher, Mr. Adams, wasn't having it. Simply because she was a girl.

Still psyched to become a pilot, Yvonne decided to major in mechanical engineering in college.

Hold your horses, her parents said.

Not about mechanical engineering but about going to college right after high school. When she graduated, she'd be sixteen. Too young for college, her parents felt.

At age eighteen, Yvonne was off to Howard University in Washington, DC, where she was the lone female in its mechanical engineering department. "There were females in electrical and chemical engineering," she recalled, "because the electrical and chemical areas/departments didn't have the same stigma of 'getting dirty' as mechanical engineering had." When Yvonne graduated from Howard in 1951, she was the first black woman to hold a bachelor's degree in mechanical engineering from that school.

After that triumph and a three-month job search, petite Yvonne (about 117 pounds and five-four) landed a job at Frankford Arsenal, at that time a US Army munitions plant in Philadelphia (a first for a black woman). Months later, she moved on to a division of RCA (Radio Corporation of America), in Camden, New Jersey (another first for a black woman).

Love soon prompted Yvonne to shift gears.

In 1955 she married William Clark Jr., who taught bio-chem at Meharry Medical College in Nashville, Tennessee. Yvonne became an educator, too, at nearby Tennessee Agri-cultural & Industrial State College (now Tennessee State University—TSU). She was the first woman to teach in its engineering school.

The uniqueness and the abilities of this first-er came into wider view when the July 1964 issue of *Ebony* magazine hit the newsstands. In it was a major photoessay on the woman known professionally as "Y. Y. Clark."

"For most women in the field," the article began, "teach-ing is a daily sedate occupation. But for Yvonne Clark of Nashville, Tenn., it means keeping abreast of the latest devel-opments in jet propulsion, handling bulky gear systems and lecturing to virtually all-male classes." Her typical day, said *Ebony*, "involves delivering lectures on subjects like truss construction, demonstrating the relative strengths of metals and counseling her machine-bitten students on the growing number of careers open to them in the space age."

Y. Y. Clark was most passionate about teaching. She taught at TSU for more than fifty years—twice serving as department head (1965–1970 and 1977–1988). Along the way she became another first: the first black woman to earn a master's degree in engineering management from Nashville's Vanderbilt University (1972).

Not one for idle hands, Y. Y. kept busy most summers

problem solving for companies and government agencies. One summer she returned to Frankford Arsenal, where she tackled the problem of a ballistic weapon that kept jamming in cold weather. While her male colleagues scratched their heads, Yvonne had the good sense to enlarge a drawing of the weapon four times so that she could better see every detail.

Bingo!

"The overall tolerance was wrong and the fitting was too tight," she later explained.

Translation: two parts were too close together.

Y. Y. Clark worked for NASA some summers, too: once at its Manned Spacecraft Center in Houston, Texas. There she developed special containers used by *Apollo 11* astronauts in 1969 to bring moon rocks back with them to Earth for scientific study.

"When I came back to visit my high school after my freshman year at Howard, I went to see my teacher, Mr. Adams [who hadn't let me take the mechanical drawing class]. I told him, 'If a girl wants to take this course, you'd better let her have it.' I had entered Howard unprepared because of him. I would have done better if I had had that class in high school."

—YVONNE YOUNG CLARK

ANGELLA DOROTHEA FERGUSON

1925– • Pediatrician & Sickle Cell Anemia Researcher

I n the early 1950s this graduate of DC's Howard University College of Medicine made a painful discovery: There was very little medical research on black children. Most pediatric studies focused on children of European descent. Ferguson came to this realization shortly after she hung out her shingle as a pediatrician in DC.

▲ **SAVING THE CHILDREN:** Angella Dorothea Ferguson (second row, third from left) with fellow members of Kappa Pi Medical Society at Howard University in 1949, the year she graduated from med school. Ferguson earned a bachelor's degree in chemistry from Howard in 1945.

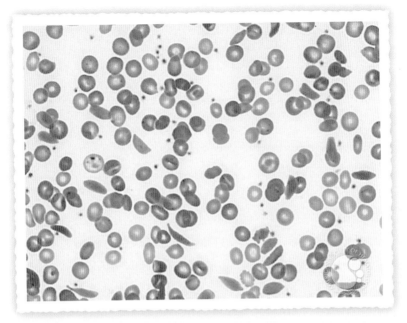

▲ **UNDER THE MICROSCOPE:** Sickle-shaped cells can be seen here in this blood sample on a microscope slide. Sickle cell anemia was first identified in the early 1900s in Walter Clement Noel, a well-to-do black man from Grenada who was studying dentistry in Chicago.

With a former professor, Roland Scott, Dr. Ferguson began intense studies of black children and their development. In the process she learned that many of them had sickle cell anemia, a hereditary condition primarily found in people of African descent.

Blood cells shaped like sickles (or crescents) have trouble bonding with oxygen, and so the vital flow of oxygen to tissues is hampered. Children with sickle cell anemia can suffer, among other things, bouts of intense pain in their joints, and even death. Dr. Ferguson gave us a better understanding of sickle cell anemia, its symptoms, its progression, and most of all its early detection. For while there is no cure, there are treatments, including blood transfusions and medications.

On May 17, 1954, while Dr. Ferguson was researching young black lives, the US Supreme Court handed down its decision in the case *Brown v. Board of Education of Topeka*. The high court ruled that segregated public schooling was unconstitutional, overturning the 1896 *Plessy* decision, which sanctioned segregation. *Brown* was a bundling of five lawsuits filed in protest of indignities and hardships black children faced because of where they were forced to attend school. The lead lawyer for the plaintiffs was the NAACP's Thurgood Marshall, a future US Supreme Court justice.

Research Marshall and his team relied on in *Brown* to demonstrate the damage segregation could do to a black child's psyche included that of psychologist **Mamie Phipps Clark** and her husband, Kenneth Clark, also a psychologist. In their study (the "dolls test") black children were presented with a doll that looked like them and one that looked like a white child. The majority of the black children associated negative things (like being bad) with the black doll. When asked which doll they wanted to play with, the majority chose the white doll. Their self-esteem was that messed up.

Mamie Phipps Clark, a native of Hot Springs, Arkansas, had earned her bachelor's and master's degrees in psychology from DC's Howard University (1938 and 1939), then a PhD in psychology from New York City's Columbia University (1943)—a first for a black woman.

JESSIE ISABELLE PRICE

1930–2015 • Veterinary Microbiologist

I n the late 1950s and early 1960s ducklings were dying at an alarming rate, mostly of *Pasteurella anatipestifer,* a bacterial disease.

Jessie Isabelle Price, a native of Montrose, Pennsylvania, identified this disease while working on her PhD at Cornell University in Ithaca, New York, completed in 1959. She then joined the research team at Cornell's Duck Research Laboratory in Eastport, Long Island, a town famous for its white Pekin duck farms. These ducks, aka Long Island ducks, were a favorite of chefs around the nation.

By 1966 Dr. Price had a vaccine that curbed the duckling death rate. She went on to develop vaccines for other avian ailments. Beginning in 1977 she worked for the National Wildlife Health Center in Madison, Wisconsin.

Microbiology, the study of living organisms invisible to the naked eye, = Greek **mīkros** (μῑκρος), meaning "small" + **bios** (βίος), meaning "life" + **logia**, a Latinization of the Greek **logos** (λόγος), meaning "the study of."

BESSIE BLOUNT

1914–2009 • Nurse, Physical Therapist,
Inventor & Forensic Scientist

On February 21, 1966, New Jersey's *Vineland Times Journal* reported: "The Soroptimist Club last week at Richards Farms was entertained with rapid character analyses from handwriting by Miss Bessie Blount of Newfield, and shown prosthetic devices she uses in her work with the physically handicapped."

This Soroptimist Club was a branch of an international union of women working for peace and the betterment of the lives of women and girls. The club's name comes from the Latin words for "sister" (*soror*) and "best" (*optima*).

When Bessie Blount was a kid in Hickory, Virginia (now Chesapeake, Virginia), she daydreamed that her best self would be someone in the medical field, helping people. That dream was a wisp in the wind. You see, Hickory didn't educate its black children beyond the sixth grade.

Thankfully, at some point in the 1920s, Bessie's mother, Mary, whose husband died during World War I, moved to New Jersey. There young Bessie had a raft of school days. It included nurse's training and culminated in studies at the Panzer College of Physical Education and Hygiene (now part of Montclair State University) in East Orange, New Jersey.

During and after World War II Bessie Blount, nurse and physical therapist, worked at hospitals for veterans. Her patients included men who had lost arms. For them she invented devices that would enable them to be a bit more independent. She later received patents for several devices to help people with disabilities. One—No. 2,550,554, patented in 1951—made it possible for paralyzed people to feed themselves.

Bessie Blount also taught her patients to write using teeth and toes, something she had mastered as a kid after a teacher rapped her knuckles (presumably with a ruler) for writing with her left hand. Back then people thought there was something wrong with being left-handed.

Bessie learned to write with her right hand, but perhaps to spite her teacher she didn't stop writing with her left hand. Not only did she become ambidextrous, young Bessie also trained herself to write with teeth and toes—and to write backward, forward, and upside down, too.

That early fascination with different ways to write

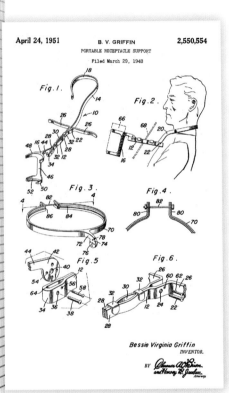

▲ HELPING PEOPLE: Blount's patent to empower paralyzed people is under her married name "Griffin," though after her marriage she was professionally known as Bessie Blount.

grew into a serious curiosity about what handwriting can reveal about people, including their mental and physical health. This led to a career as a forensic scientist. For that, Bessie took courses in handwriting analysis. A certified graphologist (handwriting expert) by 1965, Bessie lectured widely on the subject and uncovered skulduggery (mostly forgeries) for several police departments.

Said Bessie to a reporter in 1969: "If someone should try to palm off a ball pen signature on a will or other document dated prior to the invention of ball pens, for instance, we would know this was a false signature." She also claimed that in cases of twins, triplets, and such, the first-born could be identified by his or her handwriting.

In 1972 Bessie Blount became chief examiner for the Portsmouth, Virginia, police force. A few years later she undertook advanced studies in graphology in London, at Scotland Yard's document division.

Back from London, Bessie Blount started a new business: authenticating documents, including those related to slavery and US treaties with Native Americans. Her clients were mostly museums and independent researchers.

▶ **DREAMER:** Edith Lee-Payne from Detroit, Michigan, on her twelfth birthday at the March on Washington for Jobs and Freedom on August 28, 1963, where Reverend Dr. Martin Luther King Jr. delivered his famous "I Have a Dream" speech. One of the things Edith grew up to do was cofound the Lee-Lovett Foundation, an organization that encourages donations of organs and tissue especially in the black community.

PART 3

Onward!

The civil rights and black power movements of the 1950s and 1960s combined with actions by a rainbow of women in America calling for equality of opportunity, resulted in the doors to STEM fields opening up a little more to black women.

Milestone moments of the period include . . .

December 14, 1961: With Executive Order 10980, President John F. Kennedy creates the President's Commission on the Status of Women. He taps former First Lady Eleanor Roosevelt to head it. The commission's 1963 report provides irrefutable proof of major discrimination women face in the workplace.

July 2, 1964: President Lyndon B. Johnson signs into law the landmark Civil Rights Act of 1964, aimed at eradicating discrimination based on race, color, national origin, religion, and sex on many fronts, including in employment and education. With it comes the creation of the Equal Employment Opportunity Commission (EEOC), a watchdog with the power to fine companies for workplace discrimination.

August 6, 1965: President Lyndon B. Johnson signs into law the Voting Rights Act of 1965 aimed at wiping out widespread (especially in the South) use of challenges such as literary tests to keep black people from voting, from having a say.

June 30, 1966: Betty Friedan—a white woman whose 1963 book *The Feminine Mystique* about the frustrations of white middle-class housewives became a bestseller—cofounds the National Organization for Women (NOW), today the largest US feminist advocacy organization.

GEORGIA MAE DUNSTON

1944– • Geneticist

I had a curiosity about the differences in people," Georgia Mae once said, reflecting on her childhood. "Why we were different, different in skin color, why our hair was different were the questions that I often pondered."

Georgia Mae spent that childhood in Norfolk, Virginia. With her aptitude for math and science, this daughter of a working-class couple became keen on biology in junior high. Academic excellence led to a full scholarship to Norfolk State University (NSU). There she was tremendously inspired and encouraged by a biology professor, Dr. Louis Austin.

After she graduated from NSU in 1965 with a bachelor's degree in biology, Georgia Mae set out to New York City (where she had family), ready to, as she put it, "take on the world." She was brimming with confidence that she'd land a job as a laboratory technician, at a hospital perhaps, testing blood samples, for example, to aid MDs in diagnosing diseases or giving patients clean bills of health.

Georgia Mae did not get her wish.

The Big Apple was not as liberal, as racism-free, as this Southerner imagined. "I'd go for a lab tech job interview and they'd tell me that they had something in housekeeping or the job just closed."

Georgia Mae returned home ready to throw in the towel on having a career in the sciences, but then her great champion at NSU, Professor Austin, urged her to apply for a fellowship at Tuskegee Institute (now University) in Tuskegee, Alabama.

At Tuskegee, Georgia Mae thrived as she began studying genetics and earning a master's degree in biology. And here she found another great encourager: biochemist David Aminoff, a visiting professor from the University of Michigan. After she earned that master's degree in 1967, Georgia Mae was off to the University of Michigan.

In Ann Arbor, Georgia Mae had to deal with cold, cold weather.

The cold shoulder, too, at times. She was the only black student in the university's human genetics department.

Georgia Mae didn't turn tail. She persevered. In 1972 she had her PhD in human genetics—a first for a black woman.

After that, Dr. Dunston did in a way take on the world. She became a world-

▲ **SO CURIOUS:** Dr. Dunston in the January 2013 Capstone, a Howard University online publication.

class geneticist. In satisfying that childhood curiosity about the differences in people, she mostly applied her mind to the genes and immune systems of black people. She explored the genetic roots of diseases and conditions to which people of African descent are especially susceptible, such as hypertension and diabetes. Her work also included research on the trouble black people often had with organ transplants. As writer Tina Gianoulis explained, "Dunston's research uncovered the fact that, since the tests for organ matches had been created using cells from white people, they often did not work when used to test organ matches for blacks."

Dr. Georgia Mae Dunston did this work based in DC, as a professor of microbiology at Howard University's med school for more than forty years. There she established the human immunogenetics laboratory and was made head of her department in 1998.

In 2001 Dunston cofounded Howard's National Human Genome Research Center, in part to provide information on black genetics to the international Human Genome Project (HGP). Started in 1990 and completed in 2003, the HGP resulted in the identification and mapping out (or "sequencing") of the roughly twenty thousand genes in human DNA—the genome—for the purposes of better understanding what makes us who we are and also to come up with new and better cures and treatments for diseases.

After the HGP was completed, the National Institute of Health's National Human Genome Research Institute entered into partnership with Dr. Dunston's genome research center. The goal was, among other things, to step up the research on diseases that especially afflict people of African descent and to increase black participation in medical studies.

Genetics, the study of heredity, derives from the Greek **genetikos** (γεννητικός): "generative, productive."

Immunogenetics is a subset of genetics that focuses on the relationship between genetics and the immune system, a body's defense system against viruses and other harmful things.

JOAN MURRELL OWENS

1933–2011 • Marine Biologist

The year was 1970.

Joan, a wife and mother, was an educator with a bachelor's degree in fine arts from Fisk University (1954, where she double minored in mathematics and psychology). She also held a master's degree in guidance counseling (specializing in reading therapy) from the University of Michigan (1956).

And Joan, thirty-seven, was ready to change course—follow her first bliss.

When she was a child in Miami, Florida, family pastimes included wondrous fishing trips. Joan fell in love with marine life—especially corals—and she daydreamed of becoming a marine biologist. She later relished such books as *The Silent World* by French oceanographer Jacques Cousteau and *Lady with a Spear*, the autobiography of the half-Asian, half-white American marine biologist Eugenie Clark (aka the "Shark Lady"). Both books were published in 1953.

Seventeen years later, when Joan decided to pursue marine science, she enrolled in George Washington University in DC. Three years later this geology major (with a minor in zoology) had a bachelor of science degree. Three years after that, a master's (again in geology with a minor in zoology).

▲ **IT'S NEVER TOO LATE:** This photograph of Joan Murrell Owens accompanied the article "Six Variations On the Scientific Quest" in a 1989 issue of *New Directions*, a Howard University journal.

Joan then went to work on a PhD. While doing that, she taught in Howard University's geology and geography department.

In 1984 Joan had that PhD in geology—a first for a black woman—and became an expert on button corals: rather mysterious doughnut-shaped creatures of the deep, deep, deep sea (where light never penetrates). Unlike reef corals, button corals don't bunch up together but lead solitary existences.

Joan discovered a new genus (category or group) and two species (genus members) in an already known genus. She named one species *Letepsammia franki* after her husband, Frank Owens, who had cheered her on when she decided to change course in 1970.

LETEPSAMMIA FRANKI: A species of button coral Joan Murrell Owens named after her husband, Frank.

"You ask me the question, 'What is this research on deep water solitary corals good for?' Well, it's not going to make anybody rich; it's not going to be a cure for cancer; it's not going to lead to anything like that. But it's knowledge. It's information. It's information, in particular, that provides insights into our 'last frontier,' the Earth's oceans . . .

You can't foresee where that knowledge might lead. The more man knows, maybe the better he'll behave in terms of preserving his world, and the more he might see an analogy that he can use for himself." —JOAN MURRELL OWENS

Joan once said that she was "programmed to enter science." Indeed, she had a slew of science minds in her family, several of them women. They include first cousin Carolyn Beatrice Parker (see page 62) and second cousin Muriel E. Poston, a botanist. The science-minded men include Joan's father, William Murrell, a dentist, and uncle Julius Parker, a physician.

JUNE BACON-BERCEY

1932– • Meteorologist

On June 2, 1977, the *Washington Post* had this to say: "On June 20, at 8 p.m., on Channel 5, all of Washington can watch June Bacon-Bercey go down to defeat at the hands of a Chinese watchmaker from Forrest City, Ark."

No, this wasn't about a rerun of a sporting event but a match of minds on a trivia game show playoff. The show was *The $128,000 Question*. That Chinese watchmaker's category was Big Bands. June Bacon-Bercey's was the life and work of John Philip Sousa, best known for marching-band music.

Though June—then a resident of Silver Spring, Maryland—lost in the playoff, she had already won a whopping $64,000 (the equivalent to about $275,000 today).

Buy a yacht? Designer clothes? A Ferrari? New house?

Nah.

June didn't have *things* on her mind, but people. She told the *Washington Post* that she planned to turn most, perhaps all, of her winnings into a scholarship fund for young women who wanted to follow in her footsteps: become experts on the Earth's atmosphere, from rain and snow to typhoons and tornadoes and other winsome to worrisome ways of weather.

Wichita, Kansas, native June Bacon-Bercey, the daughter of a music teacher (mother) and an attorney (father), had a bachelor's degree in mathematics (1954) from the University of Kansas, then a master's degree in math and meteorology (1955)

▲ **WEATHER WOMAN:** June Bacon-Bercey. Date unknown.

from the University of California, Los Angeles (UCLA)—the first black woman to earn a degree in meteorology. And this was not her last "first."

Having worked for the National Meteorological Center in Washington, DC, then for the tech company Sperry Rand, in 1971 June became the first female TV meteorologist. This was at NBC affiliate WGR in Buffalo, New York, where she was also a newscaster and host of a morning show. In 1972 she became the first woman and first black person awarded the American Meteorological Society's Seal of Approval for excellence in TV weather forecasting. This trailblazer later had careers at the National Weather Service and the National Oceanic and Atmospheric Administration (NOAA).

By the way, June kept her word about that game show prize money. The first annual June Bacon-Bercey Scholarship in Atmospheric Sciences for Women, administered by the American Geophysical Union, was awarded in 1978 to Anthea J. Coster. Coster was a white graduate student in space physics and astronomy at Rice University in Houston, Texas. She became an expert on space weather.

A year after Coster received that scholarship, June had herself yet another degree: a master's in public administration from the University of Southern California in LA.

The Greek **meteōron** (μετέωρος), meaning "thing high up" + **logia**, a Latinization of the Greek **logos** (λόγος), meaning "the study of" = meteorology.

PATRICIA SUZANNE COWINGS

1948– • Psychophysiologist & Inventor

▲ **MIND-BODY WORK:** Patricia Suzanne Cowings circa 1978 at NASA's Ames Research Center in Silicon Valley.

Seven years before white physicist and engineer Sally Ride became the first US woman to enter outer space (1983) and sixteen years before engineer and physician **Mae C. Jemison** became the first black woman to do so (1992), Bronx, New York–born Patricia Cowings was the first woman enrolled in NASA's scientist astronaut training program (1976–1977). She was an alternate for a 1979 mission but never voyaged into space. With her PhD in psychology from the University of California (1973), Cowings did, however, have a terrific career at NASA.

Patricia Cowings, PhD, is best known for inventing for NASA the Autogenetic-Feedback Training Exercise (AFTE) in 1979. AFTE is a means of combating space sickness (like motion sickness), for which pharmaceuticals wouldn't work, as they might make astronauts go haywire while performing their space tasks. AFTE involves (1) a series of thirty-minute biofeedback techniques—that is, the electronic monitoring of more than twenty of a person's bodily responses to situations such as changes in heart rate and blood pressure, and (2) lessons on how to control those responses and thereby combat space sickness. AFTE took off—and not just for NASA. Among other things, it became the basis for a treatment for high blood pressure and nausea caused by chemotherapy.

MAMIE PARKER

1957– • Biologist & Environmentalist

Legendary singer-songwriter Marvin Gaye played a role in Mamie's career. His 1971 hit song "Mercy Mercy Me" truly spoke to her soul.

"He talked about the pollution in the air, and the wind that was blowing poison and radiation and all of that," Mamie told NPR's Michel Martin in 2015.

Born the year that the courageous Little Rock Nine enrolled in the once all-white Central High in Little Rock, Arkansas, Mamie was a ninth grader at the recently desegregated Wilmot High in the tiny town of Wilmot, Arkansas, when she first heard that Marvin Gaye song.

At Wilmot High Mamie was a stellar student—all As except for one B in French. She took that marvelous, mercy-oriented mind of hers to the University of Arkansas at Pine Bluff. There early on she declared herself a biology major.

It was also there that one day during her sophomore year a stranger paid her biology class a visit—a man who changed her life. He was University of Arkansas grad Hannibal Bolton, a black fishery biologist with the US Fish and Wildlife Service (USFWS).

"Who likes to fish?" Hannibal Bolton asked.

Mamie's hand shot up.

That was thanks to Mama: Cora Parker, a sharecropper who raised Mamie and her ten siblings in a four-room house not far from Lake Enterprise and the Bayou Bartholomew. Cora, a make-a-way-out-of-no-way woman, was an avid fisher (not surprising, given all the mouths she had to feed). Mama's love of fishing really rubbed off on Mamie, the youngest— and a girl fascinated with small creatures, from slithering snakes to the night crawlers she captured for her cane-pole catching of carp, catfish, bass, bowfin, and other good eats.

So although in college Mamie knew she wanted a career that would have her outdoors, she didn't have a road map until Hannibal Bolton came along. At his urging, Mamie took advantage of summer-fall USFWS internships, first

▲ **VERY DOWN-TO-EARTH:** Arkansas Hall of Famer Dr. Mamie Parker in early November 2016 in Qingdao, China, at the fifth Annual World Congress of Ocean. The topic: "Building More Diverse Partnerships in Marine Environment and Resource Protection."

in Wisconsin, at its Genoa National Fish Hatchery, then in Minnesota, at its New London Fish Hatchery. During those internships Mamie learned what it takes to raise fish for the purpose of restocking depleted lakes and streams. She also learned about how to check for fish diseases, about optimum water quality, oxygen levels, and temperatures.

After getting her bachelor's degree in biology (1980), Mamie attended the University of Wisconsin in Madison for a master's degree in fish and wildlife management, then a PhD in limnology (the study of lakes and other bodies of fresh water).

Dr. Mamie Parker became a USFWS lifer, with a nearly thirty-year pathbreaking career. Highlights include becoming the first black head of fisheries when, in 2001, she took the helm of a regional office. Her domain was the thirteen-state Northeast Region. In 2003, she became the agency's assistant director for fisheries and habitat conservation.

When Dr. Mamie Parker retired from the USFWS in 2007, she had accomplished a great deal to get people to have mercy on our environment. For one thing, she got the Atlantic salmon put on the endangered species list (1994). Beginning in 2001 and ending in 2003, she was chief negotiator with General Electric on its cleanup of the Hudson River, which the company had contaminated with toxic polychlorinated biphenyls (PCBs) for thirty years (1947–1977).

Dr. Parker was also a leading architect of the National Fish Habitat Action Plan, launched in 2006. Its mission: "to protect, restore and enhance the nation's fish and aquatic communities through partnerships that foster fish habitat conservation and improve the quality of life for the American people."

After she retired, through speaking engagements and in other endeavors, Dr. Parker didn't let up on rallying folks to have mercy on the environment—to help people understand the connection between environmental health and human health. Whenever, wherever, she kept promoting what she calls "wild-STEM."

SHIRLEY ANN JACKSON

1946– • Physicist

E very time you listen to a CD, scan an item in the grocery store, or slide a DVD into your computer, you're using technology that Shirley's work helped improve." So wrote Diane O'Connell in her biography of Shirley Ann Jackson, a book titled *Strong Force*.

Strong force is more than just a title. It is one of the primary forces addressed in the field of particle physics, the branch of science that studies the basic parts of radiation and matter and the interactions between them by looking at atoms, the building blocks of matter. Strong force is the naturally occurring binding of subatomic particles, such a protons and neutrons together in the core (or nucleus) of the atom.

Strong force is what Shirley embodied in her ascendency to acclaimed physicist, the aptitude for which was evident when she was a kid in Washington, DC.

One guiding light was a biography of Benjamin Banneker, an eighteenth-century black self-taught scientist. And young Shirley had a thing for bees and wasps. She collected them, studied them—how they reacted to light, to darkness, how they behaved when fed this or that, what happened if, say, bumblebees and yellow jackets were thrown together into the same habitat.

▲ **MAKING THE GRADE:** Shirley Ann Jackson in 1973, the year she earned her PhD in physics from MIT.

With the help of her dad, a postal worker and World War II veteran who was a natural when it came to things mathematical and mechanical, Shirley built go-carts from wood and spare parts found in her father's workshop and in the streets. She built cart after cart, experimenting with different-sized axles, for example. She played around with body designs, all in the hope of winning downhill races in a contraption propelled not by electricity or gas but by gravity alone. Even then, Shirley was attempting to understand the laws of nature.

What's more, young Shirley took to heart something her dad told her and her siblings again and again: "Aim for the stars so that you reach the treetops and at any rate you'll get off the ground." Dad's "essential message," daughter later recalled, "was if you don't aim high you won't go far."

After a stellar high school career and with her mind on mathematics, Shirley indeed went far: in 1964 to one of the world's top schools for brainiacs, the Massachusetts Institute of Technology (MIT) in Cambridge. At the time, there were only about ten black people among MIT's eight thousand students and only about forty women in her freshman class of nine hundred. Shirley and future physician **Jennifer Rudd** were the class of 1968's only black women.

Racism and sexism at times clipped Shirley's wings: "I went through a down period, but at some point you have to decide you will persist in what you're doing and that you won't let people beat you down."

And so Shirley kept aiming high. Psyched by a course she took early on—PANIC (Physics: A New Introductory Course)—she earned a bachelor's degree in physics, then aimed even higher—and made history.

In 1973 Shirley Ann Jackson had a PhD in physics. She was the first black woman to earn one from MIT and the second US black woman to earn a PhD in physics. (**Willie Hobbs Moore**, a native of Atlantic City, New Jersey, had earned hers in 1972 from the University of Michigan).

After MIT, Dr. Shirley Jackson, theoretical physicist—one who relies on mathematics to better understand and anticipate natural phenomena like strong force—did postdoctoral work at the Fermi National Accelerator Laboratory, aka Fermi-lab, a US Department of Energy unit near Chicago, Illinois, that is all about particle physics. She also did work at the world's top particle physics lab, the European Organization for Nuclear Research headquartered in Geneva, Switzerland.

In 1976 Dr. Jackson was hired by AT&T Bell Laboratories in Murray Hill, New Jersey, to work in its theoretical physics department. There she theorized on a range of things with an emphasis on solid-state physics (the study of solids),

▲ **TO THE HEIGHTS:** On May 16, 2016, President Barack Obama awarded Dr. Shirley Ann Jackson and eight other scientists the government's highest award for scientific achievement, the National Medal of Science. Jackson was the first black woman to receive this award, established in 1961. In 2009 President Obama had tapped Dr. Jackson to serve on the President's Council of Advisors on Science and Technology (PCAST).

quantum physics (the study of how electrons and other particles behave), and optical physics (the study of the characteristics of light and how it interacts with matter). For one, some of Dr. Jackson's research was on enhancing the efficacy of semiconductors (such as silicon), essential components of tons of things we rely on in our everyday lives, from refrigerators to mobile phones.

In 1991 Dr. Jackson left Bell Labs to become a professor of physics at Rutgers University in Piscataway and New Brunswick, New Jersey. Then, in May 1995, she became a commissioner of the US Nuclear Regulatory Commission, the agency charged with seeing to the safety of the nation's nuclear power plants. Shortly after she joined this commission, President Bill Clinton appointed her its chair.

In July 1999 Dr. Jackson became the first woman and the first black president of Rensselaer Polytechnic Institute, a private research university in Troy, New York, established in 1824 to train people "in the application of science to the common purposes of life."

PATRICIA E. BATH

1942– • Ophthalmologist, Laser Scientist & Inventor

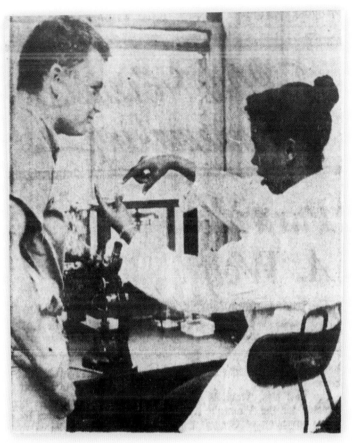

▲ **EMPOWERED:** Teenaged Patricia Bath in the August 15, 1959, *New York Age.*

In 1988 Dr. Bath, seriously science-minded as a child, received a patent for a new device.

It was the Laserphaco Probe, a device and technique for removing cataracts, clouding of the lens of an eye that can lead to blurry vision and blindness. Bath's invention (US patent No. 4,744,360) was the first laser treatment for cataracts, and she was the first US black woman MD to receive a patent for a medical device.

Bath worked on her invention for five long years, spending some of that time boning up on laser technology in Germany, at the University of Berlin. The Laserphaco Probe was not the only "first" for this native of Harlem, New York, the daughter of a man from Trinidad and a woman of African and Cherokee descent born in the States. Her parents, said Dr. Bath, were "the fuel and engine of my empowerment."

So empowered—and smart—was young Patricia that she completed high school in two and a half years instead of the usual four. What's more, while still at Charles Evans High, in the summer of 1959, she received a grant from the National Science Foundation to do research at the Albert Einstein College of Medicine of Yeshiva University in the Bronx, New York. At Yeshiva, Patricia and other

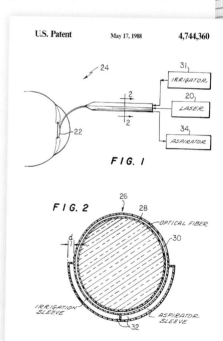

VISIONARY: From Bath's patent application for the Laserphaco Probe.

gifted teens explored the link between stress, nutrition, and cancer. Attending that summer institute was a major boost. In her 2011 induction into the American Academy of Ophthalmology's Museum of Vision, Bath said the institute "brought me closer to the reality of believing that, yes, I can achieve, yes, I will go to medical school, and yes I will achieve my dream. My NSF award and mentorship at Yeshiva was a life changing event."

The fact that the summer institute said yes to Patricia was major, too. In August 1959 the black-owned newspaper *New York Age* reported that out of the 160 high school juniors and seniors who applied to the program, sixteen-year-old Patricia was one of only 28 accepted. "A surprising element in this young lady's background," remarked the *Age,* "is the fact there is no scientific history in her family. Her interest in the field came about as a result of a very healthy 'curiosity' which took her into comprehensive reading on various scientific subjects. As Miss Bath herself explains it, 'I'm just searching for truth.'"

That curiosity, that search for truth, led *Mademoiselle* magazine to award Patricia a 1960 Merit Award, applauding her as one of the year's ten most outstanding young American women. (Another was black track-and-field star Wilma Rudolph, who won three gold medals at the 1960 Olympics in Rome.)

Next steps for Patricia?

* Bachelor's degree in chemistry from Hunter College (1964).

* MD from Howard University College of Medicine (with honors in 1968).

* Internship at Harlem Hospital (1968–1969).

* Residency in ophthalmology at New York University, completed in 1973—a first for a black person.

* Fellowship at Columbia University to do more study and training in corneal (specifically, cornea transplant) and keratoprosthesis (artificial cornea implant) surgery. By then, having discovered that in her New York City world black people had a higher rate of blindness and visual impairment than white people, she had spearheaded a now common discipline: community ophthalmology, wherein volunteer eye-care workers visit institutions, from day care centers to senior citizens' homes, to see if people need glasses and to screen for eye diseases.

After Columbia, Dr. Bath was soon off to LA to work as an assistant professor of ophthalmology at the University of California, Los Angeles (UCLA) and of surgery at nearby Charles R. Drew University (named after the black physician, surgeon, and medical researcher regarded as the "father" of the blood bank). In 1975 Dr. Bath became the first female faculty member at UCLA's Jules Stein Eye Institute, and in 1983 became the first woman in the world to head an ophthalmology residency training program, that of Drew/UCLA. By then, she had cofounded (in 1976) the American Institute for the Prevention of Blindness (AiPb), a not-for-profit organization predicated on the belief that "eyesight is a basic human right."

When it comes to all her firsts, Patricia Bath has not been prone to ego-tripping. "I wasn't seeking to be first. I was just doing my thing, and I wanted to serve humanity along the way—to give the gift of sight."

The Greek **ophthalmos** (ὀφθαλμός) meaning "eye" + **logia**, a Latinization of the Greek **logos** (λόγος), meaning "the study of" = ophthalmology.

DONNA AUGUSTE

1958– • Electrical Engineer, Computer Scientist,
Data Scientist & Entrepreneur

I first started out interested in technology when I was a kid and the Apollo space missions were broadcast on television," said Donna Auguste in a 2007 interview with the National Center for Women in Information Technology. "I was just riveted," she added. "When they would show the mission control room, I'd get as close to the TV as you could get just checking out all of the details. From that point forward I knew I wanted to be involved in computers and technology and emerging science."

Born in Beaumont, Texas, and raised in Berkeley, California, this daughter of Louisiana Creole parents had a thing as a kid for disassembling and then

▶ **AMONG THE TOP IN TECH:** Donna Auguste with the Newton, from a January 2, 1994, *New York Times* article about her. Along with becoming a force in STEM, Donna became a gospel musician (bass guitars, piano, and conga drums). Donna, who holds more than twenty patents for original inventions, has said that the source of her strength is "my relationship with God."

reassembling toasters and whatnot. With that inquisitive mind Donna earned a bachelor's degree in electrical engineering and computer science from the University of California, Berkeley (1980). Then Donna forged into a white- and male-dominated field to become the first black woman conducting research toward a PhD in computer science at Carnegie Mellon University in Pittsburgh, Pennsylvania. There, from 1981 to 1984, she did research on artificial intelligence (AI).

Donna left Carnegie Mellon before getting that PhD because an opportunity came along that she couldn't pass up: a job with a relatively new kid on the block, IntelliCorp, one of the first commercial AI firms. Donna managed a team of software engineers who implemented expert systems—that is, computer applications that make decisions using knowledge and reasoning, like human experts do.

Then came jobs with other top tech firms. One was Apple. While there, Donna managed the team that produced the Newton, one of the first mobile personal digital assistants (PDAs). The Newton paved the way for today's smartphone technology.

In 1996 Donna Auguste took a leap of faith and stepped out on her own: She cofounded Freshwater Software, Inc., in Boulder, Colorado. Freshwater offered companies cool tools to monitor their websites for reliability. Freshwater got off the ground with $250,000 from investors. After it was up and running, there was another infusion of cash ($1 million).

That's certainly a lot of money, but sustaining some start-ups can take more money than you imagine.

At one point, Freshwater had trouble staying afloat.

Faced with adversity, Donna Auguste reached deep into her toolbox for three things that had always served her well: passion, self-discipline, tenacity.

It worked. In time Freshwater had titans for clients, including Hewlett-Packard. In 2001 Freshwater was sold for a whopping $147 million.

That same year *Fortune* magazine celebrated Donna Auguste as one of the top "25 Women Who Are Making It Big in Small Business." The National Society of Black Engineers gave her its Golden Torch Award for Outstanding Women in Technology.

With Freshwater sold, Donna Auguste wasn't about to just kick back and relax. In 2000 she had founded the Leave a Little Room Foundation, a charitable organization that partners with church and community organizations around the world to provide

▲ **AT LAST:** Donna Auguste, PhD, holder of more than twenty patents, on May 9, 2019—a proud graduate of ATLAS Institute at the University of Colorado Boulder. The title of her dissertation: "A Data Science Approach to STEM (Science, Technology, Engineering and Math) Identity Research for African American Communities." (ATLAS stands for Alliance for Technology, Learning, and Society.)

people with things they desperately need, from clothing and books to homes and solar power. She went to East Africa fifteen times over the next ten years to work on projects, and also worked on projects in Mexico and Haiti.

And Donna wasn't done with tech. In 2006, in Denver, she was back in business with Alpha and Omega, a research and development firm. Among other things, Alpha and Omega worked on smartphone apps and advanced sensor technology.

No amount of money, no amount of success, could quench this woman's yearning for more learning. In 2012 she began work on a master's in information technology management from Regis University in Denver. In 2016 she entered the ATLAS Institute of the College of Engineering and Applied Science at the University of Colorado in Boulder to complete that PhD she had started more than thirty years earlier. At ATLAS, her research used AI, machine learning, and sensor technology to teach data science. Her goal is to encourage more people of color to join data science, engineering, and other STEM professions.

"I'd say the single greatest challenge has been learning to trust my intuition, especially when the stakes are high. During the years when I was growing up, I learned to pay attention to my intuition and to factor [it into] my decision-making process along with other sources."

—DONNA AUGUSTE

PAMELA McCAULEY

1963– • Industrial Engineer

At age fifteen Pamela learned that she was pregnant. Some folks wrote her off, figured she'd become another statistic—high school dropout, "welfare mom."

Pamela's parents didn't harbor such thoughts. More important, neither did Pamela. This Oklahoman was not a quitter. She not only finished high school, Pamela went to college and—after juggling motherhood, work, and studies—graduated from the University of Oklahoma in Oklahoma City with a bachelor's degree in industrial engineering (IE) in 1988.

And Pamela was game for more.

Shortly before she earned that bachelor's degree, she sounded out deans about scholarships for graduate school. She knew, for example, that the National Science Foundation (NSF) was one source. She was hungry for information about other options, opportunities.

"Well, what's your GPA?" asked one dean.

Pamela told the dean that her grade point average wasn't "very good," then added, "But my last two years are good, and I'm a very hard worker."

"If your GPA were higher, above 3.5, maybe we could help you," replied the dean, writing Pamela off as definitely not graduate school material. "But, no, I don't think that we're going to be able to do anything. After all, you're about to complete a bachelor's degree. Why don't you just go to work?"

Pamela left that dean's office angry, humiliated. But not defeated. Again, not a quitter.

She applied to the NSF. It seriously disagreed with that discouraging dean and awarded Pamela a $90,000 grant. That went a very long way in enabling her to continue at the University of Oklahoma, earning a master's degree (1990), then a PhD (in 1993), both in IE. She was the first black woman to earn a PhD in IE from the University of Oklahoma and the first black woman to earn a PhD in any engineering field in the Sooner State.

With her degrees and her penetrating mind, Pamela went on to become a world-renowned expert in ergonomics and biomechanics. Her numerous awards include the Saturn/Glamour Magazine Women Making a Difference Award, *More* magazine's Woman with MORE Award, a Society of Women Engineers Engineering Educator of the Year award, and a Distinguished Alumni Award from the University of Oklahoma.

erg from the Greek **érgon** (ἔργον), meaning "work" + **nomics**, a suffix derived from the Greek nomos (νόμος), meaning "law"= ergonomics, the science behind designing and situating equipment, for example, for a worker's maximum efficiency and safety.

The Greek **bios** (βίος), meaning "life" + **mechanikē** (μηχανική), meaning "mechanics" = biomechanics, the study of the mechanics of living beings.

Dr. Pamela McCauley's expertise has been on display in her role as a professor at Orlando's University of

Central Florida (UCF). She joined its faculty in 1993 and in 2000 became head of the university's ergonomics lab in the department of industrial engineering and management systems.

Her grit, her tenacity, her brains were also on display January 1998–July 1999 when she served as the Martin Luther King Jr. Visiting Associate Professor of Aeronautics and Astronautics at the prestigious Massachusetts Institute of Technology in Cambridge. As an educator she has primed younger minds with such courses as human engineering, systems engineering, probability and statistics for engineering, along with biomechanics and ergonomics.

▶ **DEFYING EXPECTATIONS:** Pamela McCauley, PhD, CPE (Certified Professional Ergonomist), in June 2016 at the first annual Multi-stakeholder Forum on Science, Technology and Innovation for the Sustainable Development Goals (STI Forum). The two-day event, with nearly one thousand participants from around the world, was held in New York City at the United Nations headquarters. Dr. McCauley talked about three key things nations and their policy makers can do to boost the participation of their women in the world of STI/STEM: promote and provide more robust education in STI/STEM for girls and young women; increase access to resources and networks in STI/STEM for them; and encourage the advancement of women working in STI/STEM.

The woman once a written-off pregnant teenager, once an undergrad dismissed by a dean, saw no reason that she couldn't wear more than one hat. Along with being a professor, she became a dynamic public speaker—including a motivational speaker. What's more, through her firm, T-STEM Inc., she works as an expert witness in the States and abroad in legal cases involving product liability, slips and falls, and car accidents, for example.

NASA is among the government agencies that have availed themselves of McCauley's research expertise. At one point, her UCF ergonomics lab created what she calls an "ergonomically focused" workstation for the Kennedy Space Center's launch room. "Our goal was to design a work area where engineers can work comfortably (oftentimes for up to ten hours), communicate with others, analyze information, and access the technology they need to support a launch."

In 2017 the NSF chose Dr. McCauley to head its Innovation Corps (I-Corps™). I-Corps exists to help scientists and engineers transform ideas into viable commercial products. When asked for an example, she responded with this: "An example of an idea that could become a viable product is a computer-based video game that teaches STEM education through the use of real-world scenarios and the scenarios are updated based on current events that are culturally relevant to under-represented minority students."

This dynamo has also been writing for years, authoring and coauthoring more than one hundred technical papers (example: "An 8-Factor Model for Evaluating Crew Race Performance" in a January 2008 issue of *International Journal of Sports Science and Engineering*). There's her textbook, *Ergonomics: Foundational Principles, Applications, and Technologies.* There's also her *Winners Don't Quit: Today They Call Me Doctor,* a book to inspire people, especially young women, to hold fast to their dreams, to believe in themselves, and to shoot for the stars!

TREENA LIVINGSTON ARINZEH

1970– • Biomedical Engineer

T reena Livingston Arinzeh was raised in Cherry Hill, New Jersey, by a home economics teacher (mother) and a biochemist (father).

Science was in the blood, on the brain, and Treena followed in the tradition.

✳ Bachelor's degree in mechanical engineering (1992) from Rutgers University in New Brunswick, New Jersey.

✳ Master's degree in biomedical engineering (1994) from Baltimore's Johns Hopkins University.

✳ PhD in bioengineering (1999) from the University of Pennsylvania in Philadelphia.

In 2001 Dr. Arinzeh joined the faculty at the New Jersey Institute of Technology (NJIT) in Newark, New Jersey. At NJIT she established the Tissue Engineering and Applied Biomaterials Lab and became a pioneer in the use of adult stem cells—those which can morph into different types of cells—to regenerate bones, cartilage, and spinal cords and to combat diseases. Breakthroughs include the discovery that one person's adult stem cells can be implanted into another person without the recipient's immune system rejecting them.

Dr. Arinzeh's honors and awards include a Faculty Early

Career Development award from the National Science Foundation, which came with a $400,000 research grant (2003); the Presidential Early Career Award for Scientists and Engineers (2004); and in 2013 the Black Engineer of the Year Educational Leadership Award; the New Jersey Institute of Technology Excellence in Research Prize and Medal; and New Jersey Inventors Hall of Fame Award.

To be sure, Dr. Arinzeh's surpassing joy lies not in honors and awards, but in working steadily to develop ways to help heal people's bodies. And she long knew firsthand what a debilitating illness can do to a person. She was a teen when her father suffered a stroke and became paralyzed. "Just having seen him in that condition," said Dr. Arinzeh in a 2010 interview, "I felt that there must be a way . . . to try to help those that are significantly disabled to be able to function somewhat normally in life."

▶ **FOCUSED:** "This photo was taken almost seventeen years ago when I had first joined NJIT," said Dr. Arinzeh in 2018. "One of my areas of research is bone repair. Bone, if you squeeze it, will generate electrical activity. So I was measuring the voltage in the piece of bone. This phenomenon I now use to help regenerate tissues. I design materials that also perform similarly—if you squeeze/deform them, they generate electrical pulses. This phenomenon is called piezoelectricity."

AYANNA HOWARD

1972– • Roboticist

I want to build my own bionic woman."

That was Ayanna as a child, a daughter of a math major (mother) and an engineering major (father) who grew up in Altadena/Pasadena, California.

Ayanna's big wish to build a bionic woman was inspired by the 1970s TV show *The Bionic Woman*, about the fictional Jaime Sommers, who suffered a horrible skydiving accident and was put back together with technological implants that transformed her into a superwoman—and an amazing crime fighter.

Ayanna proved to be an amazingly hard worker when it came to making a life in STEM.

* Bachelor's degree in engineering (1993) from Brown University in Providence, Rhode Island.

* Master's degree (1994), then a PhD (1999) in electrical engineering from the University of Southern California, in LA.

From 1993 to 2005 Ayanna worked at NASA's Jet Propulsion Laboratory (JPL), California Institute of Technology (Cal Tech). There she helped develop navigation systems for future Mars rovers.

In 2005 Dr. Howard joined the faculty at the Georgia Institute of Technology, where, with research funded by NASA, she headed the team that created SnoMotes, tough little

▲ **ROBO-GOOD:** Ayanna Howard in 2017 with a DARwin-OP (Dynamic Anthropomorphic Robot with Intelligence—Open Platform). This robot helps children with disabilities when it comes to their physical therapy.

robots that can do things like gather data on effects of global warming in the Antarctic. At Georgia Tech, Dr. Howard also established the Human-Automation Systems (HumAnS) lab. Later on, she led a team that designed assistive, therapeutic, and educational robots for children with special needs. Wishing to build on this work and provide such useful items to the public at large, in 2013 Dr. Howard cofounded Zyrobotics. By then Ayanna Howard, PhD, also had a master's in business administration (from Claremont University, in Claremont, California, in 2005).

Two years after the launch of Zyrobotics, Business Insider, a business news website, hailed Dr. Howard as one of the world's twenty-three most powerful women engineers.

In 2018 children were still very much on Ayanna's mind. One of her HumAnS lab projects concerned devices "augmenting the capabilities of kids with motor disabilities for an improved quality of life," she told *Forbes* magazine.

Meaning?

"For example, an exoskeleton for upper arm mobility that assists when needed lets them better interact with the world."

"I was one year out from earning my PhD and had just won my first NASA grant. I arrived at my team-kickoff meeting to find one guy sitting in the room. 'They moved the secretaries' meeting down the hall,' he said. I held out my hand and said, 'Oh, you must be so-and-so. I'm Dr. Howard. I'm running this meeting. Welcome to my team.' I smiled widely as he turned slightly red and shook my hand. I had my confidence back."

—AYANNA HOWARD

PAULA T. HAMMOND

1963– • Chemical Engineer

P aula Hammond is in pursuit of the invisible," begins a Science History Institute post. "In her lab at the Massachusetts Institute of Technology (MIT) she creates technologies so small that you cannot see them with most microscopes—that is, until they save a soldier's life on the battlefield or illuminate light bulbs using stored solar power."

Before Paula began her work at MIT she earned a bachelor's degree in chemical engineering there (1984). Then for two years she worked as a process engineer for telecommunications giant Motorola, at its facility in Fort Lauderdale, Florida. Next came a master's degree in chemical engineering from the Georgia Institute of Technology in Atlanta (1988), followed by an MIT PhD (1993) in chemical engineering. Her emphasis was on polymer science: a subset of materials science aimed at designing products and processes to improve people's lives.

Example: In 2002, eight years after she joined the MIT faculty, Hammond cofounded MIT's Institute for Soldier Nanotechnologies. She and her teammates came up with a material that, when placed on wounds, stops bleeding. She has also worked on a nano gel for a more effective way of delivering drugs into a sick person's system.

Dr. Hammond, who heads the Hammond Lab at MIT's Koch Institute for Integrative Cancer Research, was appointed

▲ **NANO WORLD:** Dr. Paula T. Hammond in her lab in 2017. She was working on a more effective way to get messenger ribonucleic acid (mRNA) into cells for improved delivery of vaccines and for diseases. mRNA is a type of RNA that carries some genetic code from DNA to help create the protein that becomes skin, for example.

head of MIT's department of chemical engineering in 2015. This was a first for both a woman and a person of color.

Her long list of honors and awards includes the Distinguished Scientist Award from the Harvard Foundation (2010), election into the National Academy of Medicine (2016) and into the National Academy of Engineering (2017), and the

American Chemistry Society's National Award in Applied Polymer Science (2018). In 2019 she was elected into the National Academy of Sciences, one of the highest honors bestowed upon a scientist or engineer.

"Chemical Engineering allows you to manipulate matter in new and exciting ways, to be able to build something truly incredible that hadn't been imagined before. By understanding how and why molecules assemble, flow, move and react together, it is possible to create, design, and control a world of things." —PAULA T. HAMMOND

By the way: Dr. Hammond, born and raised in Detroit, Michigan, didn't fall far from the tree. Make that *trees*. Her parents were public health professionals: her mother a nurse and nurse educator, her father a PhD biochemist. Paula's childhood delights included watching ants build mounds and pulling apart leaves and acorns to see how they were constructed.

The prefix **nano,** meaning "one billionth," derives from the Greek **nânos** (νᾶνος), meaning "dwarf."

ASHANTI JOHNSON

1970– • Geochemist & Chemical Oceanographer

As a kid growing up in Oak Cliff, a predominantly black suburb of Dallas, Texas, Ashanti was captivated by the award-winning TV documentary series *The Undersea World of Jacques Cousteau.*

Jacques Cousteau was a white French oceanographer, conservationist, researcher, author, filmmaker, photographer—and more—whose TV show first aired in the 1960s. Episodes include "Sharks," "Savage Worlds of the Coral Jungle," and "Sunken Treasure."

When asked as a third-grader what she wanted to be when she grew up—

The "next" Jacques Cousteau.

"He worked with people of various nationalities, who spoke with different accents, as they explored exotic underwater locations," Ashanti told the magazine *American Scientist* in 2016. "Inspired by his program, each year from third through twelfth grade, I conducted a new independent project related to the ocean."

Ashanti's parents cheered her on in her passion for the undersea world. They "supplied me with *National Geographic* magazines, took me to the Dallas Aquarium at Fair Park." Her parents also bought her volumes of *Funk and Wagnalls Encyclopedia* "to support my fascination with the sea and science."

At school?

Her teachers, "strong African American women, encouraged me to pursue my dreams, even though none of them had any experience related to oceanography or could point me to a single person of color who could serve as my role model."

Fast-forward to 1993: Ashanti was the first black person to earn a bachelor's degree in marine science from Texas A&M University (TAMU) in Galveston. Six years later, at TAMU College Station, she was the first black person to earn a PhD in oceanography and became a rarity in her field: a chemical oceanographer, one who studies the chemical components of the ocean, from marine life to ecosystems.

Ashanti's journey into Jacques Cousteau's world didn't always go swimmingly. While in graduate school she witnessed a Ku Klux Klan rally at TAMU's College Station campus. She also had to contend with a male professor who referred to her as "the little black girl." What's more, Ashanti had to be her own role model. It was not until her senior year of college that she learned of a black marine scientist. That was Ernest Everett Just, who

▲ **DEEP AND FAR:** Ashanti Johnson in 2011 at the Children's Aquarium at Fair Park in Dallas, Texas, near where she grew up.

made his mark in the early twentieth century. Thankfully, Ashanti did have white female professors who were wonderfully supportive. One was Martha Scott, who became her PhD adviser.

Surging on, Dr. Ashanti Johnson became a specialist in environmental aquatic radiogeochemistry, exploring the impact of radioactive substances on rivers, estuaries, and beaches in the vicinity of former nuclear power plants or former military bombing sites, for example. "These problems have been investigated very little," Johnson told *Black Enterprise* in 2011. "It takes a lot of dedication and is really labor intensive. You get muddy, you get wet, and at the end of the day, you're happy to have processed your samples." This was a year after Dr. Johnson received the Presidential Award for Excellence in Science, Mathematics and Engineering Mentoring—one of her many awards and honors.

Dr. Ashanti Johnson also became a lighthouse and major crusader for STEM fields—especially ocean sciences—to become as diverse people-wise as the creatures that inhabit the deep blue sea. For one thing, in 2003 she founded MS PHD'S PDMI, a networking organization for undergraduates and graduate students who want to be the next Ashanti Johnson. (MS PHD'S PDMI stands for Minorities Striving and Pursuing Higher Degrees of Success Professional Development and Mentoring Institute.)

In 2016, after more than a decade as a faculty member at several universities (including Georgia Tech and the

University of Texas at Arlington), Dr. Ashanti took the helm of a newly created school geared toward getting young people to go full STEAM (Science, Technology, Engineering, Arts, and Math) ahead: Cirrus Academy Charter School in Macon, Georgia.

In 2011 the Rhode Island School of Design took the lead in calling for art and design to be integrated into elementary and secondary school STEM studies to foster more creative thinking—thus STEAM. There's also STEMM. In some cases it stands for Science, Technology, Engineering, Mathematics, and Medicine, in others Science, Technology, Engineering, Media Arts, and Mathematics. There are also calls for STREAM: Science, Technology, Reading, Engineering, Arts, and Mathematics.

YASMIN HURD

1960– • Neurobiologist

"T"he teenage brain and the adult brain definitely differ in their sensitivity to drugs," Yasmin remarked in a 2015 interview with BrainFacts.org. "We know that the prefrontal cortex, which mediates cognition, decision-making, and impulsivity, is still developing into the mid-20s, so it's more vulnerable to drug use during adolescence."

Hurd is a cutting-edge thinker and researcher on what substance abuse does to the human brain, with a special focus on the long-term impact of marijuana abuse. She has also conducted clinical trials on the use of a chemical in marijuana to combat opioid addiction. According to the Centers for Disease Control and Prevention (CDC), 63,632 people in America died of drug overdoses in 2016. Of those deaths, 42,249 (or 66.4%) resulted from overdoses of heroin, the painkiller oxycodone, morphine, or other drugs classified as opioids.

"Substance abuse has such a huge impact on our communities, on the individual, their families, on the economy of the US," Hurd told BrainFacts.org. "If we can understand the neurobiology, we can come up with more targeted treatments."

As a child in Jamaica, West Indies, and in Brooklyn, New York, Yasmin was intensely curious about the human brain.

What makes people tick?

▲ **BRAINIAC:** Dr. Yasmin Hurd in 2018 in her office at the Addiction Institute at Mount Sinai (AIMS) in New York City.

What is amiss in the brains of those who behave strangely or badly?

That curiosity led to a bachelor's and a master's degree in biochemistry and behavior (psychology) from State University of New York (SUNY) at Binghamton.

Heeding a professor's advice, Yasmin left SUNY to complete her PhD abroad, at the Karolinska Institutet in Stockholm, Sweden, a top-tier medical school and research center. With her PhD in biomedical science (1989), Dr. Hurd was a neuroscientist at Karolinska Institute for thirteen years. When she left, she had risen to both full professor and director of graduate studies in its department of clinical neuroscience.

When BrainFacts.org interviewed Dr. Hurd in 2015, she had long since returned to the States and become a member of the Mount Sinai hospital family on Manhattan's Upper East Side. At the time she was professor of psychiatry, neuroscience, and pharmacology and systems therapeutics at Mount Sinai's Icahn School of Medicine. Hurd was also the school's Ward-Coleman Chair in translational neuroscience, which is the study of the brain and nervous system that avails itself of technological breakthroughs with the goal of developing new or better treatments for people with neurological disorders. Hurd was also director of the Addiction Institute at Mount Sinai.

In 2017 Dr. Hurd was elected to the National Academy of Medicine, a premier think tank on public health and health-related policies.

PHYLLIS A. DENNERY

1958– • Neonatologist

I n the spring of 2015, Phyllis Dennery, MD, began wearing four hats in Providence, Rhode Island: pediatrician-in-chief at Hasbro Children's Hospital; the hospital's medical director; head of the department of pediatrics at Brown University's medical school, about a mile from the hospital; and professor of molecular biology, cell biology, and biochemistry at Brown.

By then, for more than twenty years Dr. Dennery had been a tireless researcher on things that ail some of the most vulnerable human beings on the planet: newborn babies. Her specialty: helping and healing babies born with damage to their lungs.

Born in Haiti and raised in Canada, Phyllis earned a bachelor of science degree

▲ **TO THE RESCUE:** Phyllis Dennery, MD, fluent in French, Spanish, and Italian (in addition to English), in her office at Hasbro Children's Hospital in 2018. Her numerous honors and awards include election in 2014 to the National Academy of Medicine, one of the highest honors given to a health professional, and induction in 2015 into the prestigious Association of American Physicians.

from Montreal's McGill University (1980). She decided to be a neonatologist (specialist in newborns) while a student at Howard University College of Medicine, in Washington, DC. "I just thought they were so fascinating, so resilient yet so small and fragile. That made me want to practice neonatology," she recalled when interviewed for an article titled "Room to Breathe."

After she graduated from Howard (1984), Dennery embarked on a residency in pediatrics in Washington, DC, at Children's Hospital National Medical Center. Then came more rigorous training at Case Western Reserve University in Cleveland, Ohio.

Before Phyllis Dennery, MD, moved to Rhode Island, she was chief of the division of neonatology and newborn services at the University of Pennsylvania and its affiliated Children's Hospital of Philadelphia. Before that, she was head of neonatology research and associate division chief at Stanford University in Stanford, California.

Greek **neos** (νέος), meaning "new" + Latin **natus,** meaning "born" + Greek **logia**, a Latinization of the Greek **logos** (λόγος), meaning "the study of" = neonatology.

LISA D. WHITE

1961– • Geologist & Micropaleontologist

I think in any science, we're still sort of battling that image that we work alone in labs, everything we do is at a bench, and that it's very isolated." So said Lisa White, PhD, in a 2017 *Earth* magazine interview. "And something I really love about geoscience is that that's rarely been my experience," she added.

▲ **FOSSIL FUELED:** Dr. Lisa White in 2004 at the Dinosaur National Monument in Jensen, Utah.

By 2017 Lisa White was into her fifth year as director of education and outreach at the University of California Museum of Paleontology (UCMP) in Berkeley. Before that, she was professor of geology at San Francisco State University for twenty-two years, starting in 1990, and for five of those years she was an associate dean. This, 1990, was a year after she earned a PhD in earth sciences from the University of California, Santa Cruz. Her area of expertise—fossils!

But not of *T. rex* and raptors.

Her expertise is microfossils: the remains of organisms that cannot be seen with the naked eye. Diatoms, for example. Diatoms are microscopic algae, with cell walls made of silica, which when living are the source of about 25 percent of the Earth's oxygen.

In graduate school at UC Santa Cruz, Dr. White zoomed in on using diatom microfossils for dating "deep marine rock sequences around the Pacific Rim and interpreting ancient environments." As diatoms evolve over time, their shells change form. Lisa uses the changes in the shell form to distinguish different episodes of time. Diatoms, as plants living in shallow water, are sensitive to temperature and chemistry changes in the water. Dr. White and other micropaleontologists compare the fossil with the modern diatoms in the same area to interpret what environmental changes happened in the past.

Along with fossil hunting, Dr. White is passionate about getting more young people jazzed about earth sciences. From

2001 to 2008 she ran SF-ROCKS (Reaching Out to Communities and Kids with Science in San Francisco) with funding from the National Science Foundation. SF-ROCKS provided high school students with earth science field and laboratory experiences. This program morphed into METALS (Minority Education through Traveling and Learning in the Sciences) with three other universities. It ran from 2010 to 2015.

During the final year of the METALS program, Dr. White took teens on a field trip in Montana's dinosaur country. Some of these young people hailed from El Paso, Texas, others from New Orleans, Louisiana, still others from Dr. White's San Francisco Bay Area. These teens were far from geoscience whizzes—some knew zip about paleontology. "But some of the things they were finding were terrific," White recalled. "And it brought out all this great skill in them—for observing, noticing details of bones." There was one young African Americn man, De'Sean Brantley, who was "a natural." He was "always finding things." One of his finds ended up in UCMP's collection. It was a partial jaw of a hadrosaur, a plant-eating dinosaur that lived in Montana 70 million years ago.

That same year Dr. White ended up on the small screen when, in November 2015, PBS first broadcast the three-part series *Making North America*.

The Greek **palaios** (παλαιός), meaning "ancient" + Greek **on** (ὤν) meaning "creature" or "being" + Greek **logia**, a Latinization of the Greek **logos** (λόγος), meaning "the study of" = paleontology.

How did Lisa White end up in earth sciences?

This daughter of Dr. Joseph L. White, a founder of the Association of Black Psychologists, and **Myrtle Escort White**, a distinguished public health nurse, had very little interest in the sciences as a kid (though she did like to dig around in her backyard). Her path, she said, was in part "influenced by my love of landscape photography and the photographer Ansel Adams. I found myself wanting to learn more about what shaped those beautiful landscapes, and wanting to learn more about what shapes the land."

There were also young Lisa's visits to museums such as San Francisco's California Academy of Sciences near her home. Its collections of minerals, rocks, and fossils intrigued her, set her mind in motion: "I began wondering how the Earth worked."

Still, photography pulled hard when Lisa started college at San Francisco State University. To fulfill a requirement, she happened to take a geology course, which happened to be taught by a terrific instructor—and it happened to be the year the Pacific Northwest's Mount St. Helens blew (May 18, 1980), the most destructive volcanic eruption in US history. This sparked Lisa's interest in a summer internship with the US Geological Survey (USGS) in Menlo Park, California, which led to another. In her third internship, she worked on a project "involving deep marine sediments and microfossils. I was hooked on fossils as a geological specialty." The deep marine sediments came from core samples from the ocean floor off the coast of California. Together with the USGS geologists and paleontologists who were Lisa's mentors, she learned the many applications of fossils for understanding environments of the past.

Dr. Lisa D. White's fascination with microfossils has taken her on explorations not only in the Americas but also in the Far East, the Middle East, Russia, and North Africa.

▲ **TINY, TINY:** This photomicrograph (photograph taken with the use of a microscope) shows the frustules (cell walls) of fifty types of diatoms.

EMMA GARRISON-ALEXANDER

1959– • Cybersecurity Professional

Emma Garrison-Alexander had a job as soon as she earned her bachelor's degree in electrical engineering from the University of Memphis in 1983.

Right out of college this native of Brownsville, Tennessee, was tapped by the National Security Agency (NSA), whose mission includes protecting America's information systems and communications networks.

Emma began her career at the NSA doing low-level programming on microprocessors and ended it as deputy for counterterrorism for Signals Intelligence (SIGINT) development.

▲ **KEEPING IT SAFE IN CYBERSPACE:** Dr. Emma Garrison-Alexander in 2016.

After twenty-five years with the NSA she went to work for another federal agency, the one charged with keeping the traveling public safe: the Transportation Security Administration (TSA). There she worked her way up to

CIO (Chief Information Officer) and assistant administrator for IT.

"Women have so much they can bring to the field—and when they get into it, they are greatly appreciated for their contributions and what they bring to the table."

—EMMA GARRISON-ALEXANDER IN A 2018 INTERVIEW WITH TECHREPUBLIC.COM ON THE "HUGE" DEMAND FOR CYBERSECURITY PROFESSIONALS

"At a day-to-day level, Garrison-Alexander's group oversees a considerable IT infrastructure supporting 70,000 government and contractor personnel," wrote Claudia Hosky in a 2012 profile. "They work at 450 airports and at 22 international locations." Garrison-Alexander ticked off for Hosky what she had to keep safe and secure from hackers. The list included:

* 17,000 desktops
* 16,000 laptops
* 7,000 smartphones
* 4,000 switches and 750 routers
* 90,000 directory mail accounts
* 2-plus petabytes (a petabyte is one million gigabytes) of data storage and tapes

So much to keep track of!
So much to keep safe!

▲ **BEWARE:** In 2018 the White House Council of Economic Advisers estimated that in 2016, evildoing cyber activities cost the US economy between $57 and $109 billion.

And by then Emma Garrison-Alexander had gotten so much more education. In 1996 she received a master of science in telecommunications management; in 2007 a PhD in management: technology and information systems track. Both degrees were from the University of Maryland University College (UMUC), in Adelphi. There in 2015 "Dr. Emma," as she is affectionately known, became vice dean of cybersecurity and information assurance at UMUC's graduate school, where she had been a faculty member of its cybersecurity program and cybersecurity policy program.

KIMBERLY BRYANT

1967– • Electrical Engineer & Founder of Black Girls Code

"his is not acceptable," Kimberly Bryant said to herself in March 2011 at a Berkeley Women Entrepreneurs conference.

Under discussion: the scarcity of black women in tech.

"Twenty-plus years after I received my engineering degree, we're still complaining that we can't find women to fill these roles. It's ridiculous."

At the time, Kimberly was working in Silicon Valley as tech manager for

▲ **LEANING IN:** Kimberly Bryant in San Francisco, California, at the 2017 Bloomberg Players Technology Summit, a gathering of topflight entrepreneurs, investors, and athletes.

pharmaceutical giant Novartis. She had done well, very well for herself. Now she wanted to do good for others—wanted to "change the equation" is how she put it.

On April 1, 2011, Kimberly Bryant launched Black Girls Code (BGC). The San Francisco–based not-for-profit offers girls of color free and affordable weekend workshops and summer camps where they can learn about computer programming, making mobile apps, and other tech tasks.

Bryant had been a tech type as a kid growing up in Memphis, Tennessee. When she enrolled in Vanderbilt University in Nashville, she was primed to become a civil engineer, but in the end she majored in electrical engineering (with minors in math and computer science).

You see, Kimberly's college days coincided with the dawn of the tech boom. The Walkman, Pac-Man, the VCR (video cassette recorder), cable TV, the personal computer, the camcorder—it was all so new. Cell phones were big clunky things that weighed about *two pounds* and cost about *four thousand dollars*. (Talk time per battery charge: a mere thirty minutes.)

Technology was where it was at! And Kimberly Bryant wanted to ride the wave. But before she could do that . . .

"Getting through Vanderbilt Engineering School was one of the hardest things I ever did in my life at the time—but it was also a great achievement," said Bryant in an interview three years after she got BGC off the ground.

What was so hard about Vanderbilt? For starters, Kimberly was one of only a few women in its engineering school. Toughing it out, she graduated in 1989. "It gave me the grit and the resiliency to be able to stick to the path I'm on right now, regardless of what the roadblocks are. I'm sticking with it to make a difference."

Kimberly Bryant has received numerous accolades for BGC. In 2013 she was one of the Champions of Change President Barack Obama honored at the White House. In 2014 the Smithsonian Institution awarded her its American Ingenuity Award in Social Progress.

In a 2014 *Smithsonian* magazine article on Kimberly Bryant, Debra Rosenberg included the voices of a host of BGC alums. Here's a sampling.

> "When I grow up, I want to be a science technologist to help people all around the world with their sicknesses."
>
> —ALEXANDRA

> "When I grow up, I aspire to become a quantum physicist."
>
> —MAI

> "I'd like to build a machine that can read my mind."
>
> —TSIA

> "I want to be an engineer and design math games for girls."
>
> —SASHA

APRILLE JOY ERICSSON

1963– • Aerospace Engineer

In 2016 Aprille Joy Ericsson became the first person of color and sixth woman to receive an award that was then a hundred years old: the Western Society of Engineers' Washington Award, given in "recognition of devoted, unselfish, and preeminent service in advancing human progress."

This award is presented annually in February during E-Week (that is, National Engineers Week), celebrated during the birthday week of George Washington, who, long before he was the first US president, was a land surveyor and an engineer.

Past recipients of the Washington Award include aviation innovator Orville Wright. On the list, too: Neil Armstrong, commander of NASA's *Apollo 11* mission, America's first to land astronauts on the moon. After touchdown, Armstrong became the first human to set foot on the lunar surface. Date: July 20, 1969.

One of Aprille's wondrous childhood memories is of four months later, on November 19, 1969. On that day, at school, she and bunch of other first graders at Brooklyn's PS 199 crowded around a small black-and-white TV a parent brought in so that they could watch the *Apollo 12* moon landing. "It broadened my horizon as a little girl growing up in the

Brooklyn hood. It helped plant that seed for dreaming about space travel." The "hood" was Bedford-Stuyvesant, or "Bed-Stuy," then a high-crime, high-poverty neighborhood.

▲ **DETERMINED:** Aprille Joy Ericsson, PhD, in the Goddard Space Flight Center's spacecraft integration and test facilities near some large Dewars (tanks used to store liquefied gases).

Star Trek, *Lost in Space*, and other sci-fi TV shows kept that dream of space travel alive in Aprille, a girl with boundless energy. At Marine Park Junior High in Brooklyn she was a member of the girls' basketball team, the school band, the science club, and the honors club, too.

Science trumped all else after Aprille won second place in the eighth-grade science fair.

And it got better!

In the summer after her junior year of high school Aprille landed a spot in an initiative now known as MITES (Minority Introduction to Engineering & Science), a seriously selective then two-week program hosted by MIT in Cambridge, Massachusetts. One of the program's sweet treats: time in a flight simulator.

With topflight grades on state and city exams Aprille could take her pick when it came to New York City's premier public high schools: Brooklyn Tech, Bronx Science, and Stuyvesant in Manhattan. "I even interviewed for Stuyvesant. However, I really liked being in Cambridge." It helped that she had family there: her maternal grandparents, the Breedys, immigrants from Barbados.

So instead of a Big Apple school Aprille attended a private school (on scholarship): the Cambridge School of Weston. This small boarding school in Weston, Massachusetts, was about a thirty-minute drive from Cambridge.

After graduating with honors from secondary school (1981), Aprille was on her way (with a scholarship) to MIT.

And to a seriously challenging time.

"The first year, calculus was the thing I kept struggling with," she told Techbridge Girls in 2015. "I passed the class, but I had to get tutoring throughout second semester. When it came to [ordinary] differential equations, it was like a major road block, I couldn't get enough of the concepts under my belt to successfully pass the course. And then I took calculus with math majors the next semester which was another mistake."

And it didn't get better.

Aprille's second year at MIT "was even tougher."

Following the advice of a very caring white professor, Sheila Widnall, Aprille made a course correction. She took a semester off and returned to New York City. There she took a calculus and two physics courses at City College.

And it got better!

She returned to MIT stronger. In May 1986 Aprille had a bachelor's degree in aeronautical/astronautical engineering. Her senior project entailed research on crew systems for spacecraft that could one day land astronauts on Mars.

Aprille graduated from MIT four months after seven American astronauts lost their lives when, seventy-three seconds after lift-off from the Kennedy Space Center in Cape Canaveral, Florida, on January 28, 1986, space shuttle *Challenger* became tragic wreckage in the sky.

The nation—the world—froze in shocked disbelief.

Though rocked by the disaster, Aprille held fast to that

childhood dream of space travel. She eventually applied to NASA's astronaut program, but an astronaut she would never be due to asthma and a knee problem. However, she would have a long, brilliant career at NASA.

It all began after she earned her master's degree in engineering from Howard University in 1992 and went to work for the NASA Goddard Space Flight Center (GSFC), in Greenbelt, Maryland. While working, she powered on at Howard University toward a PhD. In 1995 she became the first woman to earn a PhD in mechanical engineering from Howard. With that triumph, Aprille Joy Ericsson, as it turned out, was the first black woman with a PhD to be a GSFC civil servant.

Early in her GSFC career Ericsson worked on the Wilkinson Microwave Anisotropy Probe (WMAP), a satellite launched in 2001 to map the early cosmos. In time she was promoted to management positions. One of those positions was as an instrument project manager, and one of the instruments she oversaw was the Near-Infrared Spectrograph (NIRSpec) detector system for NASA's roughly $10 billion James Webb Space Telescope, successor to the Hubble Space Telescope. In 2018 the Webb observatory was on track to start orbiting the sun in 2021.

In 2014 Ericsson took on a new role: that of deputy to the chief technologist of GSFC's Applied Engineering and Technology Division. As such she oversaw nanotechnology, items like CubeSats: tiny cube-shaped satellites that typically weigh less than three pounds.

"NASA's Goddard Space Flight Center in Greenbelt, Maryland, is home to the nation's largest organization of scientists, engineers and technologists who build spacecraft, instruments and new technology to study Earth, the sun, our solar system, and the universe."

—GODDARD SPACE FLIGHT CENTER WEBSITE

When she received the Washington Award in 2016, Aprille Joy Ericsson, PhD, was NASA GSFC program manager for Small Business Innovative Research/Small Business Technology Transfer Research. Its mission: to seek out (through a proposal process) small firms worthy of grants to tackle tech problems NASA wants solved.

In January 2017 Ericsson took on the role of New Business Lead for the Instrument Systems and Technology Division (ISTD) at GSFC. ISTD exists, says NASA, "to provide specialized engineering expertise and leadership to develop state-of-the-art Earth and space science instrument hardware and innovative technologies within technical requirements and cost, on time to enable scientific discovery and exploration."

"When diversity collides it sparks innovation!"

—APRILLE JOY ERICSSON

"Our data collecting instrument subsystems expertise," Ericsson explains, "spans the entire electromagnetic spectrum," from optics and detectors to microwave sensors.

LISETTE TITRE-MONTGOMERY

1977– • Video Game Developer

I packed up and moved from Florida to San Francisco with two suitcases and my computer," Lisette told Black Girl Nerds in 2015. Lisette was talking about her quest to elevate her game about a decade earlier.

And that she definitely did.

For it was also in 2015 that Lisette made the list of *Business Insider*'s "23 of the Most Powerful Women Engineers in the World." This was fifteen years after she graduated *magna cum laude* from Miami International University of Art and Design with a bachelor of fine arts in computer animation. "Not too long after graduation," she told Black Girl Nerds, "I got my first internship working on [a] 3-D chat room game app that never went anywhere."

And so she packed those bags.

In the techie hotbed of San Francisco, Lisette landed a job as character artist at Page 44 Studios. She then went on to rise and shine in the world of video game making.

For example, from 2005 to 2011 she worked as a senior character artist at Electronic Arts (EA), where she had a big hand in the games *The Simpsons, Dante's Inferno,* and other smash hits. When interviewed by Black Girl Nerds in May 2015, she had been art manager at DeNA West (*Transformers:*

Age of Extinction) and had recently become art manager at Ubisoft SF (*Assassin's Creed*). Two years later, Lisette put on the same hat at Double Fine Productions (*Psychonauts 2*).

Where did it all start?

"I've been playing games all my life," Lisette told NPRs Michel Martin in 2013. "I've been drawing since I can remember. I think it started when I saw [the 1995 movie] *Toy Story*. It sort of clicked for me that I could be an artist and also use my left and my right brain and do very technical work, in addition to creating beautiful art."

▶ **GAME ON— AND UP:** Lisette Titre-Montgomery on the cover of *Black Enterprise* magazine (March 2011).

LATANYA SWEENEY

1959– • Computer Scientist & Data Scientist

"Y ou have zero privacy anyway," Sun Microsystems CEO
Scott McNealy famously told journalists in 1999 when
launching a new product. "Get over it."

In 2010 Facebook founder Mark Zuckerberg similarly
declared privacy dead.

Not so fast! says Latanya Sweeney. In a 2007 *Scientific American* Q&A, she insisted that there is "a primal need for secrecy
so we can achieve our goals. Privacy also allows an individual the opportunity to grow and make mistakes and really
develop in a way you can't do in the absence of privacy,
where there's no forgiving and everyone knows what everyone else is doing."

When that *Scientific American* piece appeared, Latanya
had a bachelor's degree (*cum laude*) in computer science from Harvard (1995), a master's degree in electrical engineering and computer science (1997) from
nearby Massachusetts Institute of Technology (MIT), and
a PhD in computer science from MIT (2001)—a first for a
black woman.

The year that Latanya Sweeney earned her PhD was also
the year that she founded the Data Privacy Lab at Carnegie Mellon University in Pittsburgh, Pennsylvania, which
moved to Harvard in 2011. This lab has engaged in all sorts
of problem solving, from how to crack down on fraudulent

emails (ScamSlam Project) to how to maintain DNA privacy (Genomic Privacy Project).

Sweeney's lab is perhaps best known for k-anonymity: a way for, say, a hospital to share your medical data with a scientific researcher without that researcher (or anyone else) *ever* being able to discover your identity. Her work was recognized in the 2003 HIPAA Privacy Rule enacted to strengthen privacy protections around people's health care, from medical records to health care plans. (HIPAA stands for the Health Insurance Portability and Accountability Act.)

Sweeney also master-minded the computer pro-gram Identity Angel (2006). This baby surfed the net in search of the four pieces of information a crook needs to get "Operation Identity Theft" going on a person: name, address, date of birth,

▲ **GUARDIAN ANGEL:** Dr. Latanya Sweeney in September 2017 at a congressional hearing in her capacity as a member of the CEP (Commission on Evidence-Based Policymaking) created in 2016. CEP's mission was to "develop a strategy for increasing the availability and use of data in order to build evidence about government programs, while protecting privacy and confidentiality." Dr. Sweeney's awards include the 2014 Louis D. Brandeis Privacy Award (the "Nobel Prize" of privacy awards).

and social security number. If Identity Angel hit pay dirt, it sent people friendly emails alerting them to the fact that they were at risk of identity theft. It also advised on next steps.

In that 2007 *Scientific American* Q&A Sweeney explained that years earlier she had discovered that "if I had the date of birth, gender and a five-digit zip code of a person, I could identify 87 percent of the people in the United States. So even if you don't give me your social security number, I can find out who you are nearly nine out of ten times." She also said that after the launch of Identity Angel, she was shocked to discover how many people put their social security numbers on résumés they posted online.

In her mission to keep privacy alive, Sweeney not only works on privacy-enhancing technologies but also encourages other techies to think about privacy when designing technology. And she urges the general public to think about the privacy they give up—what data about themselves they surrender in their embrace of technology (often because they don't read the fine print).

A favorite example turns on two bits of body monitoring tech: the Apple Watch and the Sleep Number bed. With the Apple Watch, the data about, say, your heart rate is stored on that device and on the iPhone you may have connected to that watch. It remains completely under your control. By contrast, data gathered by a Sleep Number bed is stored on that company's servers, and the company owns any data gathered on anyone who uses that bed.

"We do live in a technocracy. The design of the technology and how it works is really sort of the new policy," Sweeney told the audience during her keynote address, "Saving Humanity," at the 2018 first conference for Fairness, Accountability, and Transparency (FAT).

By then, this cofounder and former codirector of the PhD program in computation, organizations, and society at Carnegie Mellon University's School of Computer Science and former chief technology officer at the US Federal Trade Commission had been a professor of government and technology at Harvard University since 2012.

And Latanya Sweeney, PhD, was still going strong in her mission, as her website states, "to create and use technology to assess and solve societal, political and governance problems, and to teach others how to do the same."

PATRICE BANKS

1980– • Mechanic

▲ **#sheCANic:** Patrice Banks in her garage in August 2018. The admitted red-high-heel shoe-a-holic does not necessarily recommend repairing cars in high heels.

Patrice, raised in Phoenixville, Pennsylvania, had always been one smart cookie. With a bachelor's degree in materials engineering from Lehigh University in Bethlehem, Pennsylvania (2002), she had a successful career as a materials engineer and manager at the mega science and tech firm

DuPont, headquartered in Wilmington, Delaware. But when it came to her car . . .

This brilliant Materials Girl was, she confessed, an absolute "auto airhead." Patrice was totally intimidated by male mechanics. Unable to find a woman mechanic in the Philadelphia area where she lived, she became the woman she was looking for.

In 2011, at age thirty-one, Patrice started taking night classes in automotive technology at the Delaware Technical Community College—"I was the only girl with a bunch of boys, 19-year-old boys," she told NPR's Terry Gross. Two years later, Patrice had her mechanic's license.

After that, and with some real-world experience at Philly car repair shops under her belt, in 2016 Patrice Banks opened the Girls Auto Clinic (GAC) in Upper Darby, Pennsylvania. GAC soon made news as a female-staffed shop that caters to women—and one with a Clutch Beauty Bar where customers can get manis, pedis, and more while their vehicles are being serviced. With GAC Patrice Banks also launched a #sheCANic movement to stem the tide of female auto airheads.

"Materials engineers develop, process, and test materials used to create a wide range of products, from computer chips and aircraft wings to golf clubs and biomedical devices. They study the properties and structures of metals, ceramics, plastics, composites, nanomaterials (extremely small substances), and other substances in order to create new materials that meet certain mechanical, electrical, and chemical requirements." —BUREAU OF LABOR STATISTICS

AOMAWA SHIELDS

1975– • Astronomer & Astrobiologist

When I was twelve, I saw the movie *SpaceCamp*, about a bunch of kids who accidentally get launched into space," Aomawa Shields—her name is pronounced Ah-OH-muh-wah—told *Glamour* magazine in 2016. "That afternoon I plotted my entire career trajectory: a PhD in astronomy from MIT, followed by a job at NASA. I was like, 'I'm in.'"

Things didn't go exactly as planned.

After she graduated from Phillips Exeter Academy in New Hampshire, this native of Berkeley, California, did go to MIT and left with a bachelor's degree in earth, atmospheric, and planetary sciences (1997). After that, she began work toward a PhD in astrophysics from the University of Wisconsin in Madison.

Boom!

She hit a wall: "I just didn't fit in. I loved wearing lipstick and watching movies; everyone else seemed so serious and focused on just astronomy. It didn't help that I was the only African American woman in my department."

Aomawa left Wisconsin to pursue another passion: acting, for which she got a master of fine arts from UCLA (2001). Her acting credits include the 2005 film *Nine Lives* (under her maiden name Aomawa Baker).

As for Aomawa's life, the stars still called.

And they were aligned for her.

Through an acquaintance she met Neil deGrasse Tyson, the most famous black astrophysicist on the planet. When he learned of her celestial dreams deferred, Dr. Tyson essentially told Aomawa, "You go, girl!"

And that's exactly what she did—went back to school to become that astronomer her young self longed to be. While earning her doctorate, she made some star-related TV appearances—hosting, for example, several episodes of *Wired Science*.

In 2014 Aomawa had her PhD, a dual one—astronomy and astrobiology—from the University of Washington in

▲ **ALL-STAR:** Dr. Aomawa Shields on January 9, 2019, in Seattle, Washington, during the Plenary Lecture at the 233rd meeting of the American Astronomical Society.

Seattle. With a fellowship from the National Science Foundation she did postdoctoral work at the University of California, Los Angeles (UCLA) and at the Harvard-Smithsonian Center for Astrophysics in Cambridge, Massachusetts.

While at UCLA Shields led a team of astronomers in a study on the likelihood of a particular planet being habitable. The planet is Kepler-62f, about 40 percent larger than Earth and some 1,200 light-years away in the constellation Lyra. Kepler-62f is one of five planets that make up a planetary system discovered in 2013 by NASA's Kepler mission. Working with computer simulations and calculating various scenarios of Kepler-62f's orbit and atmosphere . . .

Verdict?

Kepler-62f might well be habitable. "We found there are multiple atmospheric compositions that allow it to be warm enough to have surface liquid water," reported Shields in 2016. "This makes it a strong candidate for a habitable planet."

"On our planet, where there's water, there's life," Shields explained earlier, in a 2015 TED Talk. "So we look for planets that orbit at just the right distance from their stars [to be] warm enough for water to flow on their surfaces as lakes and oceans where life might reside."

In 2017 Dr. Shields became an assistant professor in the department of physics and astronomy at the University of California, Irvine. That same year the NASA Habitable Worlds program said *Yes!* to her proposal to study how light

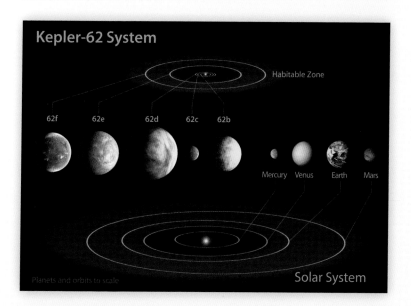

▲ **IN LYRA:** An artist's rendering of the Kepler-62 system. Like Kepler-62f, which Dr. Shields researched, Kepler-62e may also be habitable.

is absorbed or reflected by planets orbiting dim M dwarfs, aka red dwarfs, aka diminutive stars: ones that do not burn brightly and cannot be seen by the naked eye, not even on the clearest night.

With her NASA grant, Dr. Shields embarked on a three-year mission to discover what the climates are like on planets that orbit dim M dwarfs. Can they sustain life?

By then Dr. Shields, her mind on the next generation, had launched Rising Stargirls, "dedicated to encouraging girls of all colors and backgrounds to learn, explore, and discover the universe."

171

OMEGA

Rebecca Davis Lee Crumpler would be beyond proud of the strides black women have made in STEM since she became the first US black woman MD in 1864.

What a rousing "Brava!" she'd offer the twenty-first-century rising stars in STEM.

Women such as Philadelphia-born spintronics pro **Jami Valentine**. In 2006 Jami became the first black woman to earn a PhD in physics and astronomy from Johns Hopkins University in Baltimore, Maryland.

There's New Yorker **Erika Gibson**, the first US black woman board-certified veterinary neurosurgeon (2008), along with cosmologist **Chanda Prescod-Weinstein**—in 2010 this

▶ **POS·SI·BIL·I·TIES:** An unidentified twenty-first-century possible pioneer in a science lab.

LA native became one of the most recent of more than sixty US black women to earn a PhD in physics (from the Perimeter Institute for Theoretical Physics and the University of Waterloo, both in Waterloo, Ontario, Canada).

Also worthy of applause is software engineer **Brittney Katherine Exline** of Colorado Springs, Colorado. Reading at age *two* and attending the sixth grade at age *eight,* in 2007 fifteen-year-old Brittney made history as the youngest US black female accepted into an Ivy League school. That school was the University of Pennsylvania (UPenn) in Philadelphia. In May 2011 nineteen-year-old Brittney made history again as the youngest US black engineer and the youngest student to graduate from UPenn. (If that were not enough, in addition to English, she speaks Arabic, French, German, Japanese, Russian, and Spanish.)

And there's **Jedidah Isler**, raised in Niagara Falls, New York, and Virginia Beach, Virginia. In 2014 she became the first US black woman to earn a PhD in astrophysics from Yale University in New Haven, Connecticut. (Her astro-passion: blazars, short for blazing quasars).

In 2013 **Victoria Temitope Okuneye** of Brooklyn Park, Minnesota, earned a bachelor's degree in brain and cognitive sciences (with minors in chemistry and applied international studies) from MIT. After that, this daughter of Nigerian immigrants headed west to the University of Chicago's Pritzker School of Medicine for a dual degree, an MD/PhD: a medical degree and a doctorate. In her case a PhD in computational neuroscience, also known as mathematical neuroscience: the study of the brain via mathematical concepts and tools.

Mareena Robinson Snowden, a native of Miami, Florida, who as a kid recoiled from math and science, is yet another woman Dr. Crumpler would celebrate. In 2018 Mareena became the first woman of color to earn a PhD in nuclear engineering from MIT.

While celebrating Jami, Erika, Chanda, and others, Dr. Crumpler would no doubt lament that black women still make up a *tiny* percentage of Americans in a host of STEM fields. For example, in 2018 *Black Enterprise* magazine ran an article with the scary title "Are Black Women Engineers on the Brink of Extinction?" In it, writer Caroline V. Clarke reported that in 2015 black women earned a mere 1 percent of engineering degrees in America. She then added, "and that number has declined since 2011."

Dr. Crumpler, not one to despair, would no doubt respond to such stats by rallying twenty-first-century US black girls to get busy changing the equations.

"We need you! … We need your ideas. We need your innovation. We need your creativity."

—MAREENA ROBINSON SNOWDEN IN A SHOUT-OUT TO GIRLS WITH THE "SMALLEST INCLINATION TOWARD SCIENCE OR ENGINEERING" AT THE 2018 BLACK GIRLS ROCK! AWARDS.

NOTES

For complete citations for sources heavily consulted, please see Selected Sources on page 195.

ALPHA

1 **"because science and math . . . connection among them":** Eleanor Chute, "STEM Education Is Branching Out," *Pittsburg Post-Gazette*, February 10, 2009, www.post-gazette.com/news /education/2009/02/10/STEM-education-is-branching-out /stories/200902100165. Last accessed September 10, 2018.

PART 1: IN THE VANGUARD
REBECCA DAVIS LEE CRUMPLER

9 **"Soft Bones . . . Brain Fever":** Rebecca Crumpler, *A Book of Medical Discourses: In Two Parts* (Boston: Cashman, Keating & Co., Printers, 1883), pp. 127, 137, 139, 142.

9 **On Crumpler's entrance into med school:** Some sources say she entered NEFMC in 1860 but she is listed, along with twenty-one other women, as a student in the 1859–1860 term on page 4 of the *Eleventh Annual Report of the New-England Female Medical College* (Boston: Published by the Trustees, 1860).

9 **On American physicians in 1860:** Henry Louis Gates Jr. and Evelyn Brooks Higginbotham, eds., *African American Lives* (New York: Oxford University Press, 2004), p. 198.

10 **"OBGYN training . . . at the time:":** Edgar B. Herwick III, "The 'Doctresses Of Medicine': The World's 1st Female Medical School Was Established in Boston," WGBH News, November 4, 2016, news.wgbh.org/2016/11/04/how-we-live /doctresses-medicine-worlds-1st-female-medical-school-was -established-boston. Last accessed August 8, 2018.

11 **"desiring a larger scope . . .":** Rebecca Crumpler, *A Book of Medical Discourses*, p. 2.

12 **"Hospitals would not admit her patients . . . deplorable conditions":** Edgar B. Herwick III, "The 'Doctresses Of Medicine.'"

12 **"renewed vigor":** Rebecca Crumpler, *A Book of Medical Discourses*, p. 2–3.

13 **"a very pleasant . . . and gray hair":** "Sets in Colored Society," *Boston Daily Globe*, July 22, 1894, p. 29.

13 **"usefulness with the sick . . .":** Rebecca Crumpler, *A Book of Medical Discourses*, p. 1.

REBECCA J. COLE

14 **On the Institute for Colored Youth's Exam:** "1862 Final Examination Question," Institute for Colored Youth in the Civil War Era, Classes of 1856–1864, Villanova exhibits. library.villanova.edu/institute-colored-youth/their-own -words/1862-final-examination-questions. Last accessed August 8, 2018.

HALLE TANNER DILLON JOHNSON

16 **"an unusually severe . . . with a high average":** "A Colored Female Doctor," *New York Times*, September 22, 1891, p. 1.

16 **"Differentiate Pneumonia, Pleuritis, . . .":** The Alabama State Board of Medical Examiners, August 1891, "The Examination Papers in the Case of Halle Tanner Dillon, M.D.," p. 54.

ELIZA ANNA GRIER

18 **Letter to WMCP; "respectable . . . adequate means of support";**
Grier's letter to Susan B. Anthony; and Susan B. Anthony's
letter to WMCP: "Letter from Eliza A. Grier to . . . Woman's
Medical College of Pennsylvania," "Letter from Clara Marshall
to O. W. Whitaker," "Letter from Eliza Anna Grier to Susan B.
Anthony" all at doctordoctress.org/islandora/object
/islandora%3A971. Last accessed August 8, 2018.

18 **"Letter from Susan B. Anthony to Woman's Medical College":**
doctordoctress.org/islandora/object/islandora%3A1856
/record/islandora%3A2078. Last accessed August 8, 2018.

MARY ELIZA MAHONEY

22 **On rigor of the training course:** Dr. Kelly A. Spring, "Mary Eliza
Mahoney 1845–1926," National Women's History Museum,
www.womenshistory.org/education-resources/biographies
/mary-mahoney. Last accessed October 26, 2018.

SARAH E. GOODE

23 **"stair builder":** 1880 United States Federal Census (online
database). Last accessed at ancestry.com on October 26, 2018.

JOSEPHINE SILONE YATES

24 **"The aim of all true education . . .":** Jeannette E. Brown, *African
American Women Chemists*, p. 16.

IDA GRAY NELSON ROLLINS

26 **"served all races . . . children":** De Witt S. Dykes Jr., "Ida Gray
Nelson Rollins," in Jessie Carney Smith, ed., *Notable Black
American Women Book 11*, (New York: Gale Research, 1996), p. 497.

26 **statistic on dentists in 1900:** Brian K. Shue and Harriet F. Seldin, "California Women in Dentistry: A Look Back," *Journal of the California Dental Association*, January 2017, p. 18.

ALICE AUGUSTA BALL

29 **"clearly demonstrates her ability":** Illingworth's endorsement attached to Alice Ball, *The Chemical Constituents of Piper Methysticum or The Chemical Constituents of the Active Principle of the Ava Root*, scholarspace.manoa.hawaii.edu /handle/10125/1844. Last accessed October 26, 2018.

31 **on Alice's cause of death:** Several sources say that her original death certificate was altered to present the cause of death as tuberculosis. The death certificate I received from the Washington Board of Health, Bureau of Vital Statistics, states that the cause of death was "removal of tonsils—excessive inhalation of chlorine gas." It named "chronic asthma" as a contributing factor. Oddly, while the certificate gives her parents' correct names (and home address), Alice is identified as white.

ANNA LOUISE JAMES

33 **On the Brooklyn College of Pharmacy's class of 1908:** "Fifty-Three Pharmacists Receive Their Degrees," *Brooklyn Daily Eagle*, May 22, 1908, Picture and Sporting Section, p. 8.

33 **James's diploma:** Papers of Anna Louise James, 1874–1991, Series I. Personal and Biographical, 6f. Re: education. Copy of diploma from Brooklyn College of Pharmacy, 1908, Schlesinger Library, Radcliffe Institute, Harvard University.

33 **"In the five years of my business . . .":** Gregory Bond, "Recovering and Expanding Mozella Esther Lewis's Pioneering History of African-American Pharmacy Students, 1870–1925," *Pharmacy in History*, Vol. 58, No. 1–2 (2016), p. 13.

PART 2: RIDING THE WAVE

37 **"oldest documented photograph":** Diann Jordan, *Sisters in Science*, p. 4.

WILLA BEATRICE BROWN

41 **"When Willa Brown . . . wanted to see me" and "a rather frail craft . . . frightening":** Enoch P. Waters, *American Diary: A Personal History of the Black Press.* Chicago: Path Press, 1987, p. 196.

43 ***Pittsburgh Courier* coverage of Brown's exam and "I shall work next fall . . . passengers for pay":** "Young Woman Flyer Gets Pilot's License," *Pittsburgh Courier*, July 2, 1938, p. 11.

GEORGIA LOUISE HARRIS BROWN

51 **"excelled in ten subjects":** Anat Falbel and Roberta Washington, "Georgia Louise Harris Brown," pioneeringwomen.bwaf.org /georgia-louise-harris-brown. Last accessed October 26, 2018.

ANGIE LENA TURNER KING

53 **"I had it tough"; "black ——"; and "anything like that I could get":** Wini Warren, *Black Women Scientists in the United States*, p. 149.

53 **on early tragedies in Angie's life:** Some sources say that her father died shortly after her mother died. But the 1920 US Federal Census has an entry for a William Turner of McDowell County, where Angie was born. This widowed man, a laborer at a coal company, was heading a household that included two daughters, Angie and Sylvia (ages sixteen and ten), and a son, Irving (age twenty).

54 **"a wonderful teacher . . .":** Wini Warren, *Black Women Scientists in the United States*, p. 141.

MYRA ADELE LOGAN

56 "We practice together because . . . a pediatrician next door": Sidney Fields, "She Seeks Out Cancer," *New York Daily News,* July 23, 1964, p. 53.

FLEMMIE KITTRELL

58 "She was really that teacher . . .": "was not too alert . . ."; and "But have you thought of home economics? . . . women know all about it": Wini Warren, *Black Women Scientists in the United States,* pp. 154–55.

60 "Kittrell redesigned the program . . .": Charles W. Carey Jr., *African Americans in Science,* volume 1, p. 134–35.

61 "home economics was the science of living": Wini Warren, *Black Women Scientists in the United States,* p. 166.

61 "No country . . .": Wini Warren, *Black Women Scientists in the United States,* p. 168.

MARIE MAYNARD DALY

67 "was aware of . . . ": Margaret W. Rossiter, "The ~~Matthew~~ Matilda Effect in Science," *Social Studies of Science* 23, no. 2, May 1993, pp. 336–37.

ANNIE EASLEY

74 "My first bit of advice . . .": "Introducing . . .," *Science and Engineering Newsletter,* Spring 1982, p. 6.

YVONNE YOUNG CLARK

75 "I always liked to build . . . things around the house": Diann Jordan, *Sisters in Science,* p. 55.

75 "the furnace stoker to the toaster": Mary Bradby, "Yvonne Clark: Mechanical Engineering Professor at Tennessee State," *US Black Engineer,* Fall 1989, p. 24.

75 **"I was Annie Oakley"**: Carol Lawson, "Oral-History: Yvonne Young Clark and Carol Lawson," ethw.org/Oral-History :Yvonne_Young_Clark_and_Carol_Lawson. Last accessed December 11, 2018.

76 **"where she built . . ."**: Diann Jordan, *Sisters in Science*, p. 54.

76 **"There were females in electrical . . . 'getting dirty' as mechanical engineering had"**: Diann Jordan, *Sisters in Science*, p. 56.

77 **"For most women in the field . . . in the space age:** "Tenn. State's Lady Engineer," *Ebony*, July 1964, p. 75.

78 **"The overall tolerance . . ."**: Mary Bradby, "Yvonne Clark: Mechanical Engineering Professor at Tennessee State," *US Black Engineer*, Fall 1989, p. 23.

78 **"When I came back to visit my high school . . ."**: Diann Jordan, *Sisters in Science*, p. 56.

BESSIE BLOUNT

83 **"The Soroptimist Club . . ."**: "Handwriting Expert Visits Soroptimists," Vineland Times *Journal,* February 21, 1966, p. 12.

85 **"If someone should try . . . false signature"**: "Handwriting Expert to Assist Police," *Vineland Times Journal*, June 27, 1969, p. 9.

PART 3: ONWARD!
GEORGIA MAE DUNSTON

91 **"I had a curiosity . . . often pondered"**: Diann Jordan, *Sisters in Science*, p. 94.

91 **"take on the world"**: Diann Jordan, *Sisters in Science*, p. 95.

91 **"I'd go for a lab tech job interview . . ."**: Diann Jordan, *Sisters in Science*, p. 96.

93 **"Dunston's research uncovered . . .":** Tina Gianoulis, "Georgia
Mae Dunston Biography—Began to Look for Answers, Studied
Human Biology, Discovered Genetics, Returned to the Black
Community," biography.jrank.org/pages/2401/Dunston
-Georgia-Mae.html. Last accessed October 28, 2018.

JOAN MURRELL OWENS

97 **"programmed to enter science":** Wini Warren, *Black Women
Scientists in the United States*, p. 209.

97 **"You ask me the question . . .":** Harriet Jackson Scarupa,
"Six Variations on the Scientific Quest," *New Directions*,
October 1, 1989, dh.howard.edu/cgi/viewcontent
.cgi?article=1512&context=newdirections. Last accessed
April 26, 2019.

JUNE BACON-BERCEY

98 **"On June 20, at 8 p.m. . . .":** Levey, Bob, "Marching with
Sousa to $64,000," *Washington Post*, June 2, 1977, www
.washingtonpost.com/archive/local/1977/06/02/marching
-to-64000-with-john-philip-sousa/4bc2b9de-7076-4ac1-9cf1
-a0dddd90fb17/?noredirect=on&utm_term=.b8f5593aa460.
Last accessed August 20, 2018.

MAMIE PARKER

103 **"He talked about the pollution":** Michel Martin, "From Fishing
with Mom to Becoming a Top Fisheries Official," www.npr
.org/2015/07/14/421141198/from-fishing-with-mom-to
-becoming-a-top-fisheries-official. Last accessed August 7, 2018.

103 **On grades in high school:** Tonya Bolden, Interview with
Mamie Parker, August 22, 2018.

103 **"Who likes to fish?"** John Bryan, "Pioneers: Dr. Mamie Parker," www.fws.gov/fisheries/pdf_files/pioneers_dr_mamieparker.pdf. Last accessed August 7, 2018.

105 **On duties during internships:** Tonya Bolden, Interview with Mamie Parker, August 22, 2018.

106 **"to protect, restore and enhance . . .":** "Our Mission," National Fish Habitat Partnership, www.fishhabitat.org/about /action_plan/national-fish-habitat-action-plan-2nd-edition. Last accessed October 28, 2018.

106 **"wild-STEM":** Tonya Bolden, Interview with Mamie Parker, August 22, 2018.

SHIRLEY ANN JACKSON

107 **"Every time you listen to a CD . . .":** Diane O'Connell. *Strong Force*, p. 71.

108 **"Aim for the stars . . . won't go far":** Brian Lamb, "A Q&A with Shirley Ann Jackson," C-SPAN, December 10, 2004, www.c-span.org/video/?184740-1/qa-shirley-ann-jackson. 00:08:59. Last accessed February 4, 2019.

109 **"I went through a down period . . .":** Joan Oleck, "Shirley Ann Jackson 1946—," Contemporary Black Biography, Thomas Gale, 2005, www.encyclopedia.com/people/history/historians -miscellaneous-biographies/shirley-ann-jackson-american -physicist. Last accessed February 4, 2019.

111 **"in the application of science . . .":** RPI History, www.rpi.edu /about/history.html. Last accessed February 4, 2019.

PATRICIA E. BATH

113 **"the fuel and engine of my empowerment":** Martha Davidson, "Innovative Lives: The Right to Sight: Patricia Bath,"

March 3, 2005, invention.si.edu/innovative-lives-right -sight-patricia-bath. Last accessed August 14, 2018.

114 **"brought me closer to the reality . . .":** "Conversation Between Patricia Bath, MD, and Eve J. Higginbotham, MD," Orlando, FL, October 23, 2011, The Foundation of the American Academy of Ophthalmology Museum of Vision & Ophthalmic Heritage, www.aao.org/Assets/faca82f2-d78e-4844-862e -171431aac204/636430635852570000/higginbotham-and-bath -pdf?inline=1. Last accessed August 14, 2018.

114 *New York Age* **article on Bath:** Robert O. Gottlob, "Scientific Research Claims Patricia Bath's Attention," *New York Age*, August 15, 1959, p. 12.

116 **"eyesight is a basic human right":** American Institute for the Prevention of Blindness www.blindnessprevention.org /index.php. Last accessed August 14, 2018.

116 **"I wasn't seeking to be first . . .":** Christina Coleman, "'The Narrative of Surprise Has to Change:' Patricia Bath, Inventor of Laserphaco Cataract Surgery, on Black Women Making History," *Essence*, September 8, 2017, www.essence.com /news/patricia-bath-inventor-laserphaco-surgery-time-firsts. Last accessed August 14, 2018.

DONNA AUGUSTE

117 **"I first started out interested in . . . computers and technology and emerging science"; "my relationship with God";** and **"I'd say the single greatest challenge . . .":** Lucy Sanders and Larry Nelson, "Interview with Donna Auguste," National Center for Women in Information Technology www.ncwit.org/audio /interview-donna-auguste. Last accessed August 14, 2018.

PAMELA MCCAULEY

121 **Exchange with dean:** Pamela McCauley Bush, *Winners Don't Quit*, p. 239.

124 **"ergonomically focused . . . to support a launch":** Email to Author, January 30, 2019.

124 **"An example of an idea . . .":** Email to Author, January 30, 2019.

TREENA LIVINGSTON ARINZEH

127 **"This photo was taken almost . . . is called piezoelectricity":** Email to Author, December 13, 2018.

127 **"Just having seen him . . . somewhat normally in life":** TheGrio, "TheGrio's 100: Treena Livingston Arinzeh, Getting the Root of Stem Cell Science," February 1, 2010, thegrio.com/2010/02/01/thegrios-100-treena-arinzeh. Last accessed December 10, 2018.

AYANNA HOWARD

128 **"I want to build my own bionic woman":** M'Shai Dash, "Interview with Roboticist Dr. Ayanna Howard," BlackSciFi.com, April 15, 2016, blacksci-fi.com/interview-with-roboticist-dr-ayanna-howard. Last accessed October 28, 2018.

130 **"augmenting the capabilities of kids . . . better interact with the world":** Alex Knapp, "Robotics Legend Ayanna Howard on the Future of Human-Robot Interactions," *Forbes*, February 28, 2018, www.forbes.com/sites/alexknapp/2018/02/28/robotics-legend-ayanna-howard-on-the-future-of-human-robot-interactions. Last accessed October 28, 2018.

130 **"I was one year out from earning my Ph.D . . .":** Ayanna Howard, "Building the Bionic Woman," *Science*, October 9, 2014, www.sciencemag.org/careers/2014/10/building-bionic-woman. Last accessed October 28, 2018.

PAULA T. HAMMOND

131 **"Paula Hammond is in pursuit . . . solar power"**: "Paula Hammond," Science History Institute, www.sciencehistory .org/historical-profile/paula-hammond. Last accessed October 29, 2018.

133 **"Chemical Engineering allows you to . . ."**: Paula T. Hammond, research website, cheme.mit.edu/profile/paula-t -hammond. Last accessed October 29, 2018.

ASHANTI JOHNSON

134 **"'next' . . . role model"**: Ashanti Johnson and Melanie Harrison Okoro, "How to Recruit and Retain Underrepresented Minorities," *American Scientist*, March–April 2016, www .americanscientist.org/article/how-to-recruit-and-retain -underrepresented-minorities. Last accessed August 9, 2018.

135 **"the little black girl"**: "Black History Month: Dr. Ashanti Johnson," FoxNews, February 18, 2016, video.foxnews.com /v/4762903470001/?#sp=show-clips. Last accessed August 9, 2018.

136 **"These problems have been . . . your samples"**: Marcia Wade Talbert "5 Top Black Women in STEM," *Black Enterprise*, March 1, 2011, www.blackenterprise.com/women-in-stem. Last accessed June 26, 2018.

YASMIN HURD

138 **"The teenage brain . . . during adolescence"**: Teal Burrell, "Meet the Researcher: Yasmin Hurd: Marijuana and the Young Brain," BrainFacts.org, February 19, 2015, www.brainfacts.org /In-the-Lab/Meet-the-Researcher/2015/Yasmin-Hurd-Marijuana -and-the-Young-Brain. Last accessed October 31, 2018.

138 **CDC statistics:** "Overdose Deaths Involving Opioids, Cocaine, and Psychostimulants—United States, 2015–2016," Centers for Disease Control, March 30, 2018, www.cdc.gov/mmwr/volumes /67/wr/mm6712a1.htm. Last accessed October 31, 2018.

138 **"Substance abuse . . . targeted treatments":** Teal Burrell, "Meet the Researcher: Yasmin Hurd: Marijuana and the Young Brain," op. cit.

PHYLLIS A. DENNERY

142 **"I just thought they were . . .":** Kris Cambra, "Room to Breathe," Brown Medicine, www.brownmedicinemagazine.org/blog /article/room-to-breathe. Last accessed October 31, 2018.

LISA D. WHITE

143 **"I think in any science . . . rarely been my experience":** Thea Boodhoo, "Down to Earth with: Paleontologist Lisa D. White," *Earth*, September 1, 2017, www.earthmagazine.org/article /down-earth-paleontologist-lisa-d-white#bio. Last accessed August 13, 2018.

144 **"deep marine rock sequences . . . ":** Gretchen Kell, "PBS Special to Feature Berkeley Paleontologist," Berkeley News, November 2, 2015, news.berkeley.edu/2015/11/02/pbs-special-to-feature -berkeley-paleontologist. Last accessed August 13, 2018.

145 **"But some of the things they were . . . always finding things":** Thea Boodhoo, "Down to Earth with: Paleontologist Lisa D. White," op. cit.

146 **"influenced by my love of landscape photography . . .":** "Lisa White, PhD—Assistant Director for Education and Public Programs, University of California Museum of Paleontology, www.onlineeducation.com/women-breaking-barriers /interviews/dr-lisa-white. Last accessed August 13, 2018.

146 **"I began wondering how the Earth worked":** Lisa D. White, "Each One Teach One: A Geoscience Call to Action During Black History Month," January 31, 2018, fromtheprow.agu.org /one-teach-one-geoscience-call-action-black-history-month. Last accessed August 13, 2018.

146 **"involving deep marine sediments . . .":** Gretchen Kell, "PBS Special to Feature Berkeley Paleontologist," Berkeley News, November 2, 2015, news.berkeley.edu/2015/11/02/pbs -special-to-feature-berkeley-paleontologist. Last accessed August 13, 2018.

EMMA GARRISON-ALEXANDER

149 **"Women have so much . . .":** Alison DeNisco Rayome, "A Former TSA and NSA Executive Reveals How to Break into the Cybersecurity Field," TechRepublic.com, February 14, 2018, www.techrepublic.com/article/a-former-tsa-and-nsa-executive -reveals-how-to-break-into-the-cybersecurity-field. Last accessed October 31, 2018.

149 **"At a day-to-day level . . . 22 international locations"** and **what she oversaw at the TSA:** Claudia Hosky, "TSA's Dr. Emma: A Go-To Federal Executive," FedInsider.com, June 5, 2012, www.fedinsider.com/tsas-dr-emma-a-go-to-federal-executive. Last accessed October 31, 2018.

150 **Cost of cyber crimes to the US economy:** "The Cost of Malicious Cyber Activity to the US Economy," The Council of Economic Advisers, February 2018, www.whitehouse.gov/wp-content /uploads/2018/03/The-Cost-of-Malicious-Cyber-Activity-to -the-U.S.-Economy.pdf. Last accessed December 12, 2018.

KIMBERLY BRYANT

151 **"This is not acceptable . . . It's ridiculous"**: Lisa A. Dubois, "Kimberly Bryant, BE'89, Is Changing the Face of High-Tech with Black Girls Code," *Vanderbilt* magazine, September 26, 2014, news.vanderbilt.edu/vanderbiltmagazine/kimberly -bryant-is-changing-the-face-of-high-tech-with-black-girls -code. Last accessed August 14, 2018.

151 **"change the equation"**: Debra Rosenberg, "Could This Be the Answer to the Tech World's Diversity Problem?" *Smithsonian Magazine,* November 2014, www.smithsonianmag.com /innovation/answer-tech-worlds-diversity-problem -180953046. Last accessed August 14, 2018.

152 **"Getting through . . . to make a difference"**: Lisa A. Dubois, "Kimberly Bryant, BE'89, Is Changing the Face of High-Tech with Black Girls Code," *Vanderbilt* magazine, September 26, 2014, news.vanderbilt.edu/vanderbiltmagazine/kimberly -bryant-is-changing-the-face-of-high-tech-with-black-girls -code. Last accessed August 14, 2018.

153 **Quotes from BGC alumnae:** Debra Rosenberg, "Could This Be the Answer to the Tech World's Diversity Problem?" op. cit.

APRILLE JOY ERICSSON

154 **"recognition of devoted . . ."**: "Dr. Aprille Joy Ericsson," The Washington Award, www.thewashingtonaward.com/directory /dr-aprille-joy-ericsson. Last accessed December 10, 2018.

154 **"It broadened my horizon . . ."**: David Persons, "Dr. Aprille Ericsson Delivers Inspirational Talk at Engineering Week 2016," www.silveredge.com/dr-aprille-ericsson-delivers -inspirational-talk-at-engineering-week-2016. Last accessed August 22, 2018.

156 **"I even interviewed for Stuyvesant . . .":** Email to Author, August 21, 2018.

157 **"The first year . . . was even tougher":** Sarah Elovich, "STEM STAR Corner: Aprille Joy Ericsson, PhD, NASA," Techbridge Girls, July 30, 2015, techbridgegirls.org/index.php?id=262. Last accessed August 22, 2018.

159 **"NASA's Goddard Space Flight Center . . .":** "About the Goddard Space Flight Center," www.nasa.gov/centers/goddard/about /index.html. Last accessed February 5, 2019.

159 **"to provide specialized engineering expertise . . .":** istd.gsfc.nasa .gov. Last accessed May 15, 2019.

159 **"Our data collecting . . . electromagnetic spectrum"** and **"When diversity collides it sparks innovation!":** Email to Author, May 11, 2019.

LISETTE TITRE-MONTGOMERY

160 **"I packed up and moved . . . never went anywhere":** Lauren, "BGN's Women in Gaming Series: Lisette Titre," Black Girl Nerds, May 13, 2015, blackgirlnerds.com /bgns-women-gaming-series-lisette-titre. Last accessed November 5, 2018.

161 **"I've been playing games . . . beautiful art":** Michel Martin, "Changing the Game in Video Gaming—Tell Me More— NPR Interview," NPR.org, February 19, 2013, www .lisettetitre.com/outreach/2013/12/10/changing-the -game-in-video-gaming-tell-me-more-npr-interview. Last accessed November 5, 2018.

LATANYA SWEENEY

162 **"You have zero privacy . . . Get over it:"** Polly Sprenger, "Sun on Privacy: 'Get Over It,'" *Wired* magazine, January 26, 1999, www.wired.com/1999/01/sun-on-privacy-get-over-it. Last accessed August 24, 2018.

162 **"a primal need for secrecy . . ."** and **"if I had the date of birth, . . ."**: Chip Walter, "Privacy Isn't Dead, or at Least It Shouldn't Be: A Q&A with Latanya Sweeney," *Scientific American*, June 27, 2007, www.scientificamerican.com /article/privacy-isnt-dead/?print=true. Last accessed August 24, 2018.

163 **"develop a strategy . . ."**: "Commission on Evidence-Based Policymaking (CEP), Project Overview," Office of Planning, Research & Evaluation, www.acf.hhs.gov/opre/research /project/commission-on-evidence-based-policymaking -cepresearch. Last accessed December 12, 2018.

164 **On Apple Watch and Sleep Number bed:** Dave Gershgorn, "A Harvard Professor Thinks that Tech's True Power Comes from Design," Quartz, February 24, 2018, qz.com/1214645 /latanya-sweeney-explains-why-tech-companies-are-so -powerful. Last accessed August 24, 2018.

165 **"We do live in a technocracy . . ."**: Latanya Sweeney, "Saving Humanity," The Conference on Fairness, Accountability, and Transparency (FAT), February 23, 2018, posted on Youtube March 7, 2018, www.youtube.com/watch?v=OlK_nVOM2tc. Last accessed December 16, 2018.

165 **"to create and use technology to . . ."**: Latanya Sweeney, PhD, dataprivacylab.org/people/sweeney. Last accessed August 24, 2018.

PATRICE BANKS

167 **"auto airhead"**: Emma Eisenberg, "Meet the Disruptor: 'Shecanic' Patrice Banks," *Philadelphia Citizen*, May 24, 2016, thephiladelphiacitizen.org/shecanics -patrice-banks-girls-auto-clinic. Last accessed November 5, 2018.

167 **"I was the only girl"**: Terry Gross, "Girls Auto Clinic Owner: 'I Couldn't Find a Female Mechanic, So I Had to Learn,'" NPR Fresh Air, January 9, 1918, www.npr.org/2018 /01/09/576747854/girls-auto-clinic-owner-i-couldnt-find -a-female-mechanic-so-i-had-to-learn. Last accessed November 5, 2018.

167 **"Materials engineers develop, process . . ."**: "Materials Engineers," *Occupational Outlook Handbook*, Bureau of Labor Statistics, U.S. Department of Labor, April 13, 2018, www.bls.gov/ooh/architecture-and-engineering/materials -engineers.htm. Last accessed February 5, 2019.

AOMAWA SHIELDS

168 **"When I was twelve . . . I was like, 'I'm in'"** and **"I just didn't fit in . . ."**: Maggie Mertens, "Why I Changed My Life: Acting, Astronomy, and a One-of-a-Kind Career," *Glamour*, May 10, 2016, www.glamour.com/story/why-i-changed-my-life -acting-astronomy-and-a-one-of-a-kind-career. Last accessed November 5, 2018.

170 **"We found there are multiple atmospheric . . . for a habitable planet"**: Evan Gough, "Life on Kepler-62f?" *Universe Today*, May 27, 2018, www.universetoday.com/129174/life-kepler -62f. Last accessed November 8, 2018.

170 **"On our planet . . . life might reside":** Aomawa Shields, "How We'll Find Life on Other Planets," TED Talks, www.ted.com /talks/aomawa_shields_how_we_ll_find_life_on_other_planets /transcript?language=en. Last accessed November 8, 2018.

171 **"dedicated to encouraging girls of all colors . . .":** Rising Stargirls, www.risingstargirls.org/what-we-do. Last accessed November 8, 2018.

OMEGA

175 **"and that number has declined since 2011":** Caroline V. Clarke, "Are Black Women Engineers on the Brink of Extinction?" *Black Enterprise,* April 14, 2018, www. blackenterprise.com /black-women-engineers-brink-extinction. Last accessed November 6, 2018.

175 **"We need you! . . . toward science or engineering":** Mareena Robinson Snowden, acceptance speech at the August 26, 2018, Black Girls Rock! Awards, BET, www.bet.com/video /blackgirlsrock/2018/acceptance-speeches/girls-rock-tech -award-dr-mareena-robinson-snowden.html. Last accessed November 8, 2018.

SELECTED SOURCES

*Suitable for young readers

Brown, Jeannette E. *African American Women Chemists*. New York: Oxford University Press, 2011.

Bush, Pamela McCauley. *Winners Don't Quit: Today They Call Me Doctor*. Zephyrhills, FL: iNLife Media, 2013.

Carey, Charles W. *African Americans in Science: An Encyclopedia of People and Progress*, vols. 1 & 2. Santa Barbara, CA: ABC-CLIO, 2008.

Hardesty, Von. *Black Wings: Courageous Stories of African Americans in Aviation and Space History*. New York: Collins in association with the Smithsonian National Air and Space Museum, 2008.

Johnson, Sandra, interviewer. "NASA Headquarters Oral History Project, Edited Oral History Transcript of Annie J. Easley," www.jsc.nasa.gov/history/oral_histories/NASA_HQ/Herstory/EasleyAJ/EasleyAJ_8-21-01.htm.

Jordan, Diann. *Sisters in Science: Conversations with Black Women Scientists on Race, Gender, and Their Passion for Science*. West Lafayette, IN: Purdue University Press, paperback edition, 2006.

Lawson, Carol, interviewer. "Oral-History: Yvonne Young Clark and Carol Lawson," October 26, 2007, ethw.org/Oral-History:Yvonne_Young_Clark_and_Carol_Lawson.

*O'Connell, Diane. *Strong Force: The Story of Physicist Shirley Ann Jackson*. New York: Franklin Watts/Scholastic, 2005.

Petry, Elisabeth, ed. *Can Anything Beat White?: A Black Family's Letters*. Jackson, MI: University Press of Mississippi, 2005.

Warren, Wini. *Black Women Scientists in the United States*. Bloomington, IN: Indiana University Press, 1999.

ACKNOWLEDGMENTS

For the creation of this book and its journey out into the world, I am indebted to many people, starting with awesome members of the Abrams family: my editor Howard Reeves; editorial assistants Emily Daluga and Sara Sproull; managing editors Marie Oishi and Amy Vreeland; copyeditor Renée Cafiero (who is the reason I now know about the Matilda Effect!). Others at Abrams I'm so grateful for/to: proofreader Regina Castillo; associate art director Pamela Notarantonio; designer Steph Stilwell and freelancer Sara Corbett; associate production director Alison Gervais; associate director of School & Library marketing Jenny Choy; marketing and publicity associate Nicole Schaefer.

For prompt and helpful responses to inquiries I thank Bob Arrighi at the NASA Glenn Research Center; Brittany Foster and Chinara Tate at the Yasmin Hurd Laboratory, Addiction Institute at Mount Sinai; Annette Hemphill at T-STEM, Inc.; Matt Herbison at Drexel University College of Medicine; Alex Kasten at the University of Maryland University College; Tanya Klein at the New Jersey Institute of Technology; Sandra Lores at MIT; David Mitchell and Jackie Nemeth at Georgia Tech; Joanne Richards at Hasbro Children's Hospital; Anna Petkovich at Sterling Lord Literistic; Eisha Neely at Cornell University; Courtney Pinkard at the Alabama Department of Archives and History; Hannah Weinberg at Harvard University's Schlesinger Library; Adam Johnson at the Sindecuse Museum of Dentistry; Seth Caudill at the West Virginia State University Drain-Jordan Library; and Sonja N. Woods at Howard University's Moorland-Spingarn Research Center.

Thank you, Frances E. Ruffin, writer with a science background, for a number of assists on matters that bewildered me. And thank you, STEM-minded fellow writer for young readers Jennifer Swanson for reviewing certain entries.

Nelta Gallemore, thank so much for careful reading of the manuscript and for all the help with securing images and clearing permissions—and for coming up with alternate images when a portrait of a subject could not be obtained.

Thank you, agent Jennifer Lyons, for always going above and beyond.

Lastly, I am forever grateful to the subjects in this book who were wonderfully responsive and a joy to deal with: Treena Livingston Arinzeh, Donna Auguste, Patricia E. Bath, Phyllis A. Dennery, Aprille Joy Ericsson, Emma Garrison-Alexander, Paula T. Hammond, Ayanna Howard, Yasmin Hurd, Pamela McCauley, Mamie Parker, Aomawa Shields, and Lisa D. White.

IMAGE CREDITS

Page 5: Unidentified woman, Library of Congress. **Page 10**: New-England Female Medical College, Harvard Medical Library in the Francis A. Countway Library of Medicine. **Page 11**: Vintage Medical Bag Hand Drawing Engraving Style, iStock/channarongsds. **Pages 15, 17, 18, 20, and 21**: *The Eye and Its Appendages*, WMCP class of 1891, Eliza Anna Grier, Dr. Grier letter to Susan B. Anthony, and WMCP anatomy lab, Legacy Center Archives, Drexel University College of Medicine, Philadelphia. **Page 22**: Mary Eliza Mahoney, Photographs and Prints Division, Schomburg Center for Research in Black Culture, The New York Public Library. **Page 23**: page from Goode's patent, National Archives and Records Administration and the US Patent and Trademark Office. **Page 25**: Josephine Silone Yates, Library of Congress. **Page 27**: Rollins in Class of 1890, Image courtesy of the Sindecuse Museum of Dentistry and the University of Michigan Bentley Historical Library. **Page 27**: Rollins Report Card, 1887, Miss Ida Gray, First year transcript, Dental Department, University of Michigan 1888. Courtesy of the U-M School of Dentistry. Image from the Sindecuse Museum of Dentistry. **Page 28**: Alice Augusta Ball, University Libraries, University of Washington Special Collections, UW 39815. **Page 34**: Anna Louise James, Schlesinger Library, Radcliffe Institute, Harvard University. **Page 36-37**: Spelman students in lab, courtesy of Spelman College Archives. **Page 41**: Willa Beatrice Brown, US Air Force. **Page 46**: Salmonella, Rocky Mountain Laboratories, NIAID, NIH. **Page 47**: Euphemia Lofton Haynes, The American Catholic History Research Center and University Archives (ACUA), The Catholic University of America, Washington, DC. **Page 49**: Vet graphic, iStock/jossdim. **Page 51**: Georgia Louise Harris Brown, *Pittsburgh Courier* Archives. **Page 54**: Angie Lena Turner King, West Virginia State University, Drain-Jordan Library. **Page 57**: Myra Adele Logan, image courtesy of Louis Tompkins Wright papers, 1879, 1898, 1909-1997. H MS c56. Harvard Medical Library, Francis A. Countway Library of Medicine, Boston, Mass., permission by *BlackStar*. **Page 59**: Flemmie Kittrell, Deceased Alumni files #41-2-877. Division of Rare and Manuscript Collections, Cornell University Library. **Page 62**: Carolyn Parker, Author's Collection. **Page 64**: Marie Maynard Daly, Queens College Silhouette Yearbook, June 1942, courtesy of Queens College Libraries, Department of Special Collections and Archives. **Page 66**: Double helix, iStock/slavemotion. **Page 68**: Jane Cooke Wright, courtesy of the National Library of Medicine. **Page 73**: Annie Easley, NASA. **Page 75**: Yvonne Y. Clark, Walter P. Reuther Library, Archives of Labor and Urban Affairs, Wayne State University. **Page 79**: Angella Dorothea Ferguson, courtesy of the Moorland-Spingarn Research Center, Howard University Archives. **Page 80**: Sickle Cell, Image bank, Image # 3958 by American Society of Hematology Reproduced with permission of American Society of Hematology. **Page 85**: page from Blount patent, US Patent and Trademark Office. **Page 87**: Edith Lee-Payne. **Page 92**: Georgia Mae Dunston, courtesy of the Moorland-Spingarn Research Center, Howard University Archives. **Page 96**: Joan Murrell Owens, courtesy of the Moorland-Spingarn Research Center, Howard University Archives. **Page 97**: button coral, C. Brian Robbins, editor, Proceedings of the Biological Society of Washington, vol. 107 (1994) used by permission of Allen Press. **Page 99**: June Bacon-Bercey, American Geophysical Union (AGU), courtesy AIP Emilio Segrè Visual Archives. **Page 101**: Patricia Suzanne Cowings, Smithsonian National Air and Space Museum (NASM 97-15073). **Page 104**: Mamie Parker, photo by Pierre Bahizi, courtesy of Mamie Parker. **Page 108**: Shirley Ann Jackson, in 1973, courtesy MIT Museum. **Page 110**: Shirley Ann Jackson receiving the NMS, photo courtesy of the National Science and Technology Medals Foundation. **Page 112**: Bath as a teen, image courtesy of ancestry.com. **Page 113**: Page from Bath patent, US Patent and Trademark Office. **Page 117**: Donna Auguste in the *New York Times,* Jim Wilson/*The New York Times*/Redux. **Page 119**: Donna Auguste, Iconic Group—GradImages, courtesy of Donna Auguste. **Page 123**: Pamela McCauley, Institute for Sustainable Development/Pam Chasek. **Page 127**: Treena Livingston Arinzeh, New Jersey Institute of Technology. **Page 129**: Ayanna Howard, Rob Felt/Georgia Institute of Technology. **Page 132**: Paula T. Hammond, Bryce Vickmark Photography. **Page 135**: Ashanti Johnson, Steve McAlister Photography. **Page 139**: Yasmin Hurd, Elizabeth D. Herman. **Page 141**: Phyllis A. Dennery, courtesy of Dr. Phyllis A. Dennery. **Page 143**: Lisa D. White, courtesy of Lisa D. White. **Page 147**: diatoms, Randolph Femmer, USGS. **Page 148**: Emma Garrison-Alexander, University of Maryland University College. **Page 150**: cybersecurity graphic, iStock/matejmo. **Page 151**: Kimberly Bryant, David Paul Morris/Bloomberg via Getty Images. **Page 155**: Aprille Joy Ericsson, Kevin Allen Photo. **Page 161**: Lisette Titre-Montgomery, *Black Enterprise* magazine. **Page 163**: Latanya Sweeney, Commission on Evidence-Based Policymaking. **Page 166**: Patrice Banks, Reuter Photo. **Page 169**: Aomawa Shields, Photo by Phil McCarten, CorporateEventImages ©2019 American Astronimical Society. **Page 171**: Kepler-62 graphic, NASA. **Page 173**: Black student doing experiment in science lab, JGI/Tom Grill/Getty Images.

INDEX